ICONS 2018

The Thirteenth International Conference on Systems

April 22 - 26, 2018

Athens, Greece

ICONS 2018 Editors

Andrew Snow, Ohio University, USA
Alexander Núñez, Centro de Investigación y Desarrollo Industrial (CIDESI), México
Eloy Edmundo Rodríguez Váquez, Centro de Investigación y Desarrollo Industrial (CIDESI), México
Hugo Gámez Cuatzín, Centro de Investigación y Desarrollo Industrial (CIDESI), México

Printed from e-media with permission by:

Curran Associates, Inc.
57 Morehouse Lane
Red Hook, NY 12571

Printed by Curran Associates, Inc. (2018)

International Academy, Research, and Industry Association (IARIA)
412 Derby Way
Wilmington, DE 19810

Phone: (408) 893-6407
Fax: (408) 527-6351

petre@iaria.org

Additional copies of this publication are available from:

Curran Associates, Inc.
57 Morehouse Lane
Red Hook, NY 12571 USA
Phone: 845-758-0400
Fax: 845-758-2633
Email: curran@proceedings.com
Web: www.proceedings.com

ICONS 2018

Forward

The Thirteenth International Conference on Systems (ICONS 2018), held between April 22, 2018 and April 26, 2018 in Athens, Greece, continued a series of events covering a broad spectrum of topics. The conference covered fundamentals on designing, implementing, testing, validating and maintaining various kinds of software and hardware systems. Several tracks were proposed to treat the topics from theory to practice, in terms of methodologies, design, implementation, testing, use cases, tools, and lessons learnt.

In the last years, new system concepts have been promoted and partially embedded in new deployments. Anticipative systems, autonomic and autonomous systems, self-adapting systems, or on-demand systems are systems exposing advanced features. These features demand special requirements specification mechanisms, advanced behavioral design patterns, special interaction protocols, and flexible implementation platforms. Additionally, they require new monitoring and management paradigms, as self-protection, self-diagnosing, self-maintenance become core design features.

The design of application-oriented systems is driven by application-specific requirements that have a very large spectrum. Despite the adoption of uniform frameworks and system design methodologies supported by appropriate models and system specification languages, the deployment of application-oriented systems raises critical problems. Specific requirements in terms of scalability, real-time, security, performance, accuracy, distribution, and user interaction drive the design decisions and implementations.

This leads to the need for gathering application-specific knowledge and develop particular design and implementation skills that can be reused in developing similar systems.

Validation and verification of safety requirements for complex systems containing hardware, software and human subsystems must be considered from early design phases. There is a need for rigorous analysis on the role of people and process causing hazards within safety-related systems; however, these claims are often made without a rigorous analysis of the human factors involved. Accurate identification and implementation of safety requirements for all elements of a system, including people and procedures become crucial in complex and critical systems, especially in safety-related projects from the civil aviation, defense health, and transport sectors.

Fundamentals on safety-related systems concern both positive (desired properties) and negative (undesired properties) aspects. Safety requirements are expressed at the individual equipment level and at the operational-environment level. However, ambiguity in safety requirements may lead to reliable unsafe systems. Additionally, the distribution of safety requirements between people and machines makes difficult automated proofs of system safety. This is somehow obscured by the difficulty of applying formal techniques (usually used for equipment-related safety requirements) to derivation and satisfaction of human-related safety requirements (usually, human factors techniques are used).

The conference had the following tracks:

- Security and protection systems
- Application-oriented systems
- Advanced embedded systems and applications/services
- Dynamics and Control on Cooling Technologies

We take here the opportunity to warmly thank all the members of the ICONS 2018 technical program committee, as well as all the reviewers. The creation of such a high quality conference program would not have been possible without their involvement. We also kindly thank all the authors who dedicated their time and effort to contribute to ICONS 2018. We truly believe that, thanks to all these efforts, the final conference program consisted of top quality contributions.

We also gratefully thank the members of the ICONS 2018 organizing committee for their help in handling the logistics and for their work that made this professional meeting a success.

We hope that ICONS 2018 was a successful international forum for the exchange of ideas and results between academia and industry and to promote further progress in the area of systems. We also hope that Athens, Greece, provided a pleasant environment during the conference and everyone saved some time to enjoy the historic charm of the city.

ICONS 2018 Chairs

ICONS Steering Committee
Marko Jäntti, University of Eastern Finland, Finland
Leszek Koszalka, Wroclaw University of Technology, Poland
Mark Austin, University of Maryland at College Park, USA
Zoubir Mammeri, IRIT - Paul Sabatier University, France
Raimund Ege, Northern Illinois University, USA
Andrew Snow, Ohio University, USA

ICONS Industry/Research Advisory Committee
Gary Weckman, Ohio University, USA
Tzung-Pei Hong [洪宗貝], National University of Kaohsiung, Taiwan

ICONS 2018
Committee

ICONS Steering Committee
Marko Jäntti, University of Eastern Finland, Finland
Leszek Koszalka, Wroclaw University of Technology, Poland
Mark Austin, University of Maryland at College Park, USA
Zoubir Mammeri, IRIT - Paul Sabatier University, France
Raimund Ege, Northern Illinois University, USA
Andrew Snow, Ohio University, USA

ICONS Industry/Research Advisory Committee
Gary Weckman, Ohio University, USA
Tzung-Pei Hong [洪宗貝], National University of Kaohsiung, Taiwan

ICONS 2018 Technical Program Committee
Mehmud Abliz, Google Inc., USA
Witold Abramowicz, Poznan University of Economics, Poland
Mehmet Aksit, University of Twente, Netherlands
Mark Austin, University of Maryland at College Park, USA
Lubomir Bakule, Institute of Information Theory and Automation of the CAS, Czech Republic
Zbigniew Banaszak, Technical University of Koszalin, Poland
Ateet Bhalla, Independent Consultant, India
Francesco Bianconi, University of Perugia, Italy
Isabelle Borne, University of South Brittany | IRISA Laboratory, France
Albert M. K. Cheng, University of Houston, USA
David Cordeau, University of Poitiers, France
Fabio M. Costa, Federal University of Goias, Brazil
Peter De Bruyn, University of Antwerp, Belgium
Bayram Deviren, Nevsehir Hacı Bektas Veli University, Turkey
Yezyd Donoso, Universidad de los Andes - Bogotá, Colombia
Raimund Ege, Northern Illinois University, USA
Andras Farago, University of Texas at Dallas, USA
Francesco Fontanella, Università di Cassino e del Lazio meridionale, Italy
Miguel Franklin de Castro, Federal University of Ceará, Brazil
Marta Franova, CNRS, LRI & INRIA, Orsay, France
Matthias Galster, University of Canterbury, Christchurch, New Zealand
Christos Gatzidis, Bournemouth University, UK
Patrick Girard, LIRMM / CNRS, France
Frederic Guinand, Normandy University (Le Havre), France / Cardinal Stefan Wyszynski University in Warsaw, Poland
Said Hanafi, University of Valenciennces, France
Tzung-Pei Hong, National University of Kaohsiung, Taiwan

Table of Contents

An Empirical Analysis of Crypto-Ransomware Behavior

Jasmeen Kaur[1], Fehmi Jaafar[1, 2], Pavol Zavarsky[1]
[1] Department of Information System Security Management, Concordia University of Edmonton, Alberta, Canada
[2] Computer Research Institute of Montreal
Email: jkaur3@student.concordia.ab.ca, {fehmi.jaafar, pavol.zavarsky}@concordia.ab.ca

***Abstract*— Crypto-ransomware is a common type of malware that exploits software vulnerabilities of Internet accessible servers, end-user computers, and mobile devices. In this paper, the behavior of crypto-ransomware is empirically analyzed. We performed dynamic analysis of the ransomware in a virtual environment and the behavior of the malware represented using the data flow modeling approach. Modification of registry values and system call functions by the malware were within the scope of the analysis. The outcome of the empirical study provides a number of indicators that can be considered when assessing the effectiveness of solutions designed to prevent and detect crypto-ransomware.**

Keywords*— *Crypto-ransomware; Malware; Windows Operating System; Security Vulnerability; Execution flow.

I. INTRODUCTION

Ransomware is a malware that restricts the users from using their systems either by encrypting their system or by locking it, and to restore their functionality, attackers ask for ransom in bitcoins. What makes this malware different from traditional malware is its strong encryption. Indeed, crypto-ransomware uses strong encryption (like the Advanced Encryption Standard for 256 bit AES-256) and the decryption key is only provided after the ransom is paid [1]. Unlike other malware, ransomware immediately notifies the victim about the attack and demands ransom in crypto-currency. Ransomware payload is mainly spread by email, exploit kits, drive-by-download, social media, USB sticks, and security exploits in software.

A number of variants can be observed in the past years with different functionalities and features, which are used to exploit a maximum number of users. This study provides in-depth details of crypto-ransomware on the Windows platform, by analyzing registry activity, processes included, and generic flow of information during the attack. Recent variants of crypto-ransomware include CryptoWall, Cryptolocker, Lambda-Locker, and WannaCryptor [2]. Some of the new variants of ransomware target the Master Boot Record (MBR) of the system (a special type of boot sector at the very beginning of partitioned computer mass storage devices that holds the information on how the logical partitions, containing file systems, are organized on that medium). Ransomware is programmed in JavaScript, Hypertext Preprocessor (PHP), and PowerShell or Python. New variants of ransomware use different vulnerabilities to attack the victim like outdated versions of Flash Player. Ransomware uses exploit kits, such as the Angler Exploit Kit, to exploit vulnerabilities [2]. A large-scale ransomware attack took place on May 12, 2017, where the variant WannaCryptor exploited more than 200,000 systems. Ransomware attacks result in huge breaches of security, confidentiality, availability, and integrity of information. Our study shows the behavior of new crypto-ransomware variants by analyzing registry keys and system calls. Our purpose is to acquire a better understanding of the attack process of ransomware on Windows operating systems. By giving technical details of ransomware behavior, this study provides in-depth knowledge useful to improve mitigation and prevention methods now.

The objectives of this study are as follows:

- Analyze the behavior of ransomware on Windows Operating systems during an attack with different methods instead of using a traditional sandbox.
- Analyze the modifications made by ransomware during an attack to understand the purpose of each attack channel.
- Track the information flow during the attack.
- Suggest recommendations to improve current security mechanisms against ransomware and mitigate the risk of ransomware.

We present in this paper an empirical study of crypto-ransomware's behavior by using different real-time monitoring tools. To obtain the results, real-time attacks on target machine were performed in a virtual environment and observations were made accordingly. Furthermore, the flow of execution of malware was studied and generalized.

Section II describes related work done on ransomware. Empirical setup and methodology used in performing the crypto-ransomware behavior analysis are discussed in Section III. In Section IV, we explain the behavior of crypto-ransomware and its modification in specific operating system's files while performing an attack on the victim's machine. Dynamic-link library (DLLs) executed by crypto-ransomware are briefly discussed in section V. In Section VI, we show an execution flow of crypto-ransomware in High-Level architecture. From our empirical study, we observed some indicators of compromise. Hence, some recommendations based on results are presented in Section VII, which are expected to improve the current prevention and detection of crypto-ransomware Section VIII provides additional discussion of our findings. Finally, we conclude the paper and present future work in Section IX.

II. RELATED WORK

M. Choudhary et al. [3] discussed and analyzed the different variants from different families of ransomware and defined the characteristics of ransomware evolution. They analyzed samples on two major platforms, i.e. Windows and Android. The analysis was mainly based on monitoring the file system and registry activities by using tools like Cuckoo Sandbox on Windows and Anubis and Andrubis for Android. We expand their research by analyzing the behavior of new variants and combining the approach of dynamic and static analysis.

Sudhir Kumar Pandey and B. M. Methre [4] discussed three malware detection approaches, i.e. signature-based, anomaly-based, and specification-based. Malware analysis techniques included static malware analysis, string analysis and dynamic malware analysis. Static analysis uses a large database of already known suspicious codes, file signatures, and behavior of malware. In string analysis, the malware analyst tries to look for the malware specimen's name, user dialogue, password for backdoors, URLs, attacker's email address, libraries, different function calls, and processes. For dynamic malware analysis, a run time analysis is performed. In fact, the authors introduced a 12-stage lifecycle to analyze behavior of malware on run time that includes network surveillance and command-and-control (C&C are centralized machines that are able to send commands and receive outputs of machines part of a botnet) servers communication and peer coordination.

Scaife et al. [5] introduced an approach called CryptoDrop which focuses on monitoring user's data instead of monitoring each potential malicious software. This program analyzes user's data for any modifications and assigns threshold points to the process with any modifications. Researchers assigned the threshold to all the processes, and when any process reached a specific level of the assigned threshold, it was considered malicious and would be terminated. CryptoDrop has three primary and two secondary indicators. The three primary indicators are file type changes, similarity measurement, and Shannon entropy. Secondary indicators include deletion and file type funneling [5]. However, while analyzing all the files, this approach's performance is reduced. In addition, ransomware may include some newer files to encrypt to its list, which might not be present in the CryptoDrop database.

III. METHODOLOGY

In this section, we describe the empirical setup and tools used to carry out the empirical study. All empirical study steps were performed in a virtual environment. The objective of this study is to describe the behavior of new ransomware variants such as WannaCryptor Ransomware. Another purpose of this study is to show an attack's execution flow based on registry keys and system function. To gather this information, a virtual environment setup was developed in VMware Workstation 11.1.0 on a host machine Windows 7 Professional, 64bit. In VMware Workstation, we installed Windows 10, 64 bits which acted as the target machine. We configured the network interface for Windows 10 to HOST ONLY in order to avoid malware spreading to the host's operating system. Also, Host System was secured and protected from infection by enabling the firewall and Windows Defender. In order to monitor the infection and malware activities, we used Process Monitor, a real-time system monitoring tool installed on Windows 10. We also used some additional tools like Regshot and Wireshark to monitor the malware activities. We then collected the malicious executable files of ransomware of various families. Most of the ransomware samples were collected from VirusTotal and ViruShare malware repositories. Then, we executed malicious samples and performed a real-time attack on Windows 10. We placed some random document, images and .rar files on Windows 10 and disabled the Windows Defender and Firewall on the targeted machine to successfully execute the empirical study and monitor the behavior of crypto-ransomware.

IV. BEHAVIOR OF RANSOMWARE

This section is dedicated to explaining the behavior of ransomware when attacking the victim's machine. Ransomware encrypts the user's system using encrypting algorithms like AES, Rivest–Shamir–Adleman (RSA), or Rivest Cipher 4 (RC4) [18]. Then, it asks for a ransom in bitcoins. The main families analyzed in this study are the following: Sage Ransomware, WannaCryptor, Lambda-Locker, Hydra-Crypt, CryptoWall, and SamSam. Most of the ransomware samples exhibit similar general behavior when manipulating the Windows operating system with some different aspects. The ransomware has a similar flow of execution when infecting a system: an executable file via different delivery methods is launched into the target system during the execution, and it creates various legitimate sub-processes. Then, it communicates with Command and Control server by sending a POST request. Ransomware modifies various registry keys and executes various DLLs, which serve different purposes accordingly. After encrypting the victim's system, the ransomware deletes its executable file and shows the ransom note asking for a ransom. The ransomware mainly uses spam emails, advertisements, and vulnerability exploitation in network or applications as a delivery method. This malware can hide on the user's system for some time before execution and then start the encryption process at a very fast pace. The functionality of ransomware is explained in four phases which include: 1) the setup phase describes a number of modifications executed by a malware to set itself in the victim's system; 2) the communication phase describes the communication held during the attack to receive the encryption key; in addition, this phase identifies network related artifacts; 3) the encryption phase highlights the information regarding the encryption used in the ransomware attack; and 4) the last phase is the deletion of volume shadow copies of Windows.

A. Setup Phase

The ransomware creates some persistence keys on the victim's system to bypass a reboot. These files and keys are deleted when encryption is completed. The original executable malware creates a copy of itself and deletes the original file. Initially, the malware creates some files in the prefetch folder, which is usually created when an application runs for the first time from any location in Windows. The prefetch folder contains files used in loading the program. The path of the folder contains the file name and a hash of 8 characters added to give the malware file a unique ID: C:\Windows\Prefetch\filename-Hashvalue.pf. We observed that the malware was executed from this path.

Then, another registry value of Windows is parsed, to verify whether the system isrunning in a mode compatible to the application or not and check whether the basic functions of Terminal Services are enabled or not. Basically, in Windows operating systems, Terminal Services Configuration applications determine which user can perform actions like connect and disconnect to Terminal Service session.

After this step, the ransomware deletes the safeboot option to prevent the user from restarting the system in safe mode by reparsing the HKLM\System\CurrentControl registry key (HKEY_LOCAL_MACHINE, often abbreviated as HKLM, is one of several registry hives that make up the Windows Registry). We notified that in for all analysed ransom-ware analysed in our empirical study, they modify a registry value to change log on (HKLM\SOFTWARE\Microsoft\ WindowsNT\CurrentVersion\WinLogon). In fact, this registry value is responsible for user log on and log off. Malware changes it to malware path and filename so that it is executed at startup.

After making these changes, and before starting the encryption process on the victim's system, the ransomware collects the victim's system information like computer name, operating system, Digital Product Id, and System BIOS data. Then, it creates a hash of this information by reading the registry value (saved on HKLM\System\CurrentControlSet\Control\Computer\Name \ActiveComputerName\Compute_Name). To further the processing of crypto ransomware, a window appears on the victim's system and will keep popping up until the victim selects "yes". It also called the default cryptographic function of Windows, which is HKLM\SYSTEM \CurrentControlSet\Control\Cryptography\Configuration\Local\SSL\0002 and added a new value as shown in figure 1.

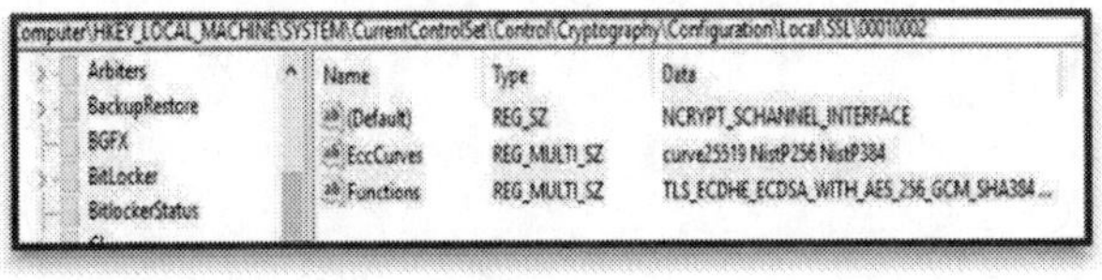

Figure 1. New value added in the Cryptography Registry key

Then, the crypto ransomware uses the Image File Execution Options (IFEO) to check if there is any active debugger. Malware also verifies whether it can attach itself to another executable like explorer.exe or svchost.exe.

B. *Communication Phase*

The ransomware tries to keep a real-time connection with the malware authors through domain and C&C Server. The malware generates a POST request to send the victim's system information to the attacker and ask to generate the domains. A UDP-based request from the victim's system is sent to thousands of Hosts. Certain packets of traffic during the attack are encrypted with RC4. In case of CryptoWall, the malware sends the POST request to the servers to get an onion address and public key to encrypt the user's system. In Figure 2, we are showing the connection attempt of a ransomware to the domain.

Class: IN (0*0001)

Time to live: 5

Date length: 34

Domain Name: lordnikom-001-qa.instavixens.net

Figure 2. Example of crypto ransomware trying to connect to the domain

The ransomware creates the registry key HKLM\SYSTEM\Current_ControlSet\Control\NetworkProvider\HwOrder to check the list of network providers. While some crypto ransomware variants use HTTP protocol, another set of them uses The Onion Router Software, (TOR) which is hard to trace as it is enabling anonymous communication. New strains of ransomware avoid using C&C servers for communication, so blocking the outbound communication does not help stopping the attack.

C. *Encryption Phase*

Encryption is the critical factor, which makes ransomware different from other malware and hard to defeat. After making a successful connection with the victim's system, the encryption phase starts. In some cases, the encryption key is generated on the victim's system. Attackers could send the key through the C&C server, but they do not share the private key. The encryption used in most of the ransomware variants is AES, RSA 2048, SHA 256, RSA-AES, which is a level 2 encryption. The ransomware uses ECDH and the Domain generation algorithms (DGA). Indeed, the Elliptic-curve Diffie–Hellman (ECDH) is an anonymous key agreement protocol that allows two parties, each having an elliptic-curve public–private key pair, to establish a shared secret over an insecure channel [20]. The DGA are algorithms seen in various families of malware that are used to periodically generate a large number of domain names that can be used as rendezvous points with their command and control servers [19]. Most of the ransomware variants add their name as an extension to every file. Ransomware payload contains a list of the files to encrypt but skips some folders like "WINDOWS", "Program Files" and "Temp" to keep the Windows System working in normal conditions. For decryption purposes, the malware keeps information about the files, like file name, size, etc. After encrypting the files, some Helper files on the victim's system are created to notify the user of the attack with instructions to pay the ransom. Most of the crypto-ransomware created files for decrypt instructions usually have the format of HTML and Text file.

D. Deletion of Volume Shadow Copies

The ransomware prevents the user from restoring the volume shadow copies by deleting them. It gains administrator rights and calls the cmd.exe to delete the Windows volume shadow copies by command: vssadmin delete shadow/all/quiet. By using this command, it deletes all the shadow copies taken by Windows without the user's knowledge. Some ransomware executes: wbadmin delete catalog-quiet to delete the shadow copies. To trace the VSS backup, a registry value was queried. Then, the ransomware changes the Windows policies depending on their functionality. For example, we observed that crypto-ransomware takes all the permissions including special permissions. In the case of WannaCryptor, system permissions are modified by using command: icacls./grantEveryone :F/T/C/Q and grant the access to Everyone. The ransomware also changes the VAD MEMORY protections to PAGEEXECUETE|PAGE_NO CACHE instead of PAGE_EXECUTE_WRITECOPY.

V. DLLs CALLED BY RANSOMWARE

A dynamic link library, DLL, is a library that contains code and data that can be used by more than one program at the same time in order to promote code reuse and efficient memory usage. During the attack, the ransomware malware uses a number of DLLs for various purposes. Some of the DLLs are generally used by other executable applications that serve a basic purpose for Windows, like Kernal32.dll, ntdll.dll, user32.dll, KernalBase.dll, python27.dll. Other major DLLs called during the malware execution were msvcrt.dll, 4ernel.appcore.dll, ws2_32.dll, Powrprof.dll, SecRuntime.dll, atl.dll, usermgrcli.dll. DLLs executed by WannaCryptor were sspicli.dll, ucrtbase.dll, rpcrt4.dll, rsaenh.dll, ntmarta.dll, uxtheme.dll, windows.storage.dll, msvcp-win.dll. It used SysWOW64 to call chkdsk.exe to check volume of disk, sector information and display the status of the drive. DLLs related to deleting the volume shadow copies are vssapi.dll and vsstrace.dll and they have some static linked DLLs, which are srcore.dll, spp.dll iasdatastore.dll.

Table I. DLLS CALLED BY CRYPTO-RANSOMWARE

DLL called	**Purposed served by DLL called**
Kernal32.dll	Used to manage process at kernel level
Mswsock.dll	Called by ransomware to manipulate another program
Urlmon.dll	Used to check the network connection
Ntdll.dll	Used to access the kernel mode from the user mode
Perfo.dll	Used to check the performance of new processes created by the malware

VI. RANSOMWARE EXECUTION FLOW

The ransomware payload is launched into the victim's system in the form of an executable. Crypto-ransomware has the code to check the availability of sandbox, any debugger or any detection technique. There are a number of processes that are called during the ransomware execution. At the execution stage, the ransomware generates a unique victim ID and key and saves it in the ".tmp" folder. When an executable is executed, it creates a legitimate process like svchost.exe or explorer.exe. In most of the variants like CryptoWall and WannaCryptor, a batch file and a copy of the original file are created. Then, the ransomware deletes itself by running a batch script.

Along with deleting the original file, the completion of the installation of a newly created copy is ensured by performing a ping request to the localhost (127.0.0.1). The malware executes conhost.exe to create multiple threads and a process with a ransom string name. Subsequently, a newly created thread under the parent process is scheduled ONLOGON, that is, even if the system restarts or any user logs on the system, this process will be executed at the run level HIGHEST. Along with ensuring its persistence, the ransomware communicates with C&C servers or generates DGA to look for the domain and dynamically change C&C servers to connect with a number of URLs. After making a successful connection, the malware attacker sends back a unique ID for each victim with the encryption key and TOR information which contains the URL for payment. WannaCryptor used TaskData\Tor\Tasksvc.exe to download the TOR information and extract this information into the Taskdata folder. Then, it creates a number of threads to change the file and directory attribute. In addition, the ransomware executed tasksche.exe to copy itself. Some of the variants executed cscript.exe to run a script from a Windows script with command "Cscript.exe//nologo .m.v". Malware collected Windows globally unique identifier (GUID), a 128-bit number used to identify information in computer systems, by querying Windows registry HKLM\SOFTWARE_Microsoft\Cryptography\Machine_Guid. This GUID is used by the malware author to know the Global Unique Identifier of the victim's system. In Figure 3, we show an example of the GUID of a system queried by a crypto-ransomware.

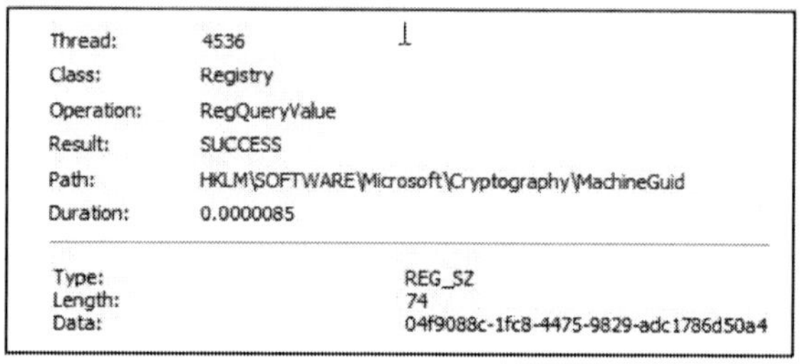

Figure 3. Example of GUID of system queried by crypto-ransomware

The ransomware notifies the victim of the attack by showing a ransom note. To manipulate the desktop wallpaper and desktop icons, the ransomware modifies the registry key HKCU\Control Panel\Desktop and performs the operation *SetInfoKey* which results in a change of the desktop wallpaper to the ransomware notification and a ransom note. Ransomware is different from other malware in that it notifies the victim of the attack and demands an amount to free the compromised system. To inform the victim of the attack, Helper Files are created within different folders of the victim's system. In fact, these Helper Files contain instructions regarding the procedure to access the onion links and pay the ransom.

After performing the whole encryption on files and folders, the ransomware deletes all its persistence keys, files and executables by calling cmd.exe, to perform an operation *Delete On Close,* which will delete the copy of the ransomware executable when it is closed.

A. In Case of Worm Functionality

Ransomware like WannaCryptor has the ability to compromise the network by scanning a number of systems in the same network. After compromising a single machine, malware attackers remotely look for other systems in the same network and deploys the payload in the network. Indeed, WannaCryptor ransomware executes its payload, creates sub processes, and runs "attrib.exe" by command attrib +h where it "hides" the directory wherever it is placed. To scan the network, it calls the GetAdapterinfo function to determine the number of IP addresses and subnet masks of the compromised system's network. This variant tries to connect with a number of domains by using API InternetOpenUrlA(). If the connection with any of the domains is successful, then payload will not execute. Otherwise, it will run the malicious payload and search for other vulnerable systems in the network on the domain.

B. New Trends of Ransomware

Many new variants of ransomware have been observed recently [6]-[10]. One of the variants offers decryption only if the victim infects two more victims and pays the ransom. Another variant performs the chkdsk, encrypts the hard disk and asks for ransom; if the victim pays, it reboots the system and encrypts the file and the victim has to pay the ransom twice. In the case of another variant called Spora, once it attacks the victim, it offers immunity from further attack. New strains of ransomware like WannaCryptor are capable of compromising numerous systems over a network, servers and databases.

Another new variant called SOREBRECT with a fileless feature is also capable of compromising a whole network [8]. This variant deletes the system's logs to delete all traces. Malicious Code utilizes Microsoft's SysInternal PsExec command-line utility for encryption, which allows the attacker to run malicious activities remotely and eliminate the need of an interactive login session or manual delivery of the malware payload into the remote machine [8]. It was also observed that the detection of this ransomware variant was only possible by analyzing abnormal behavior in the network, the RAM, and the Registry of the system.

VII. RECOMMENDATIONS

During the empirical study, most crypto-ransomware variants caused the same changes. Based on our empirical stdy and previous related work [11]-[14], we propose the following recommendations to mitigate ransomware risks:

1. It is recommended to set up a periodic and continuing strategy for data backup.
2. User awareness can reduce the risks of these attacks as not examining URLs and file extensions before opening a file is one of the common reasons of information system infections [16].
3. It was observed during the empirical study that most of crypto-ransomware variants tend to delete the Windows Volume shadow copies and any Windows backup. Therefore, any executable should not be allowed to access shadow copies of Windows and any process that tries to delete these shadow copies should be terminated.
4. Most crypto-ransomware like WannaCryptor pop up User Account Control (UAC) windows until YES is selected to gain access. Any executable with such behavior should be terminated. This signature does not apply to all the variants as some of the variants bypass this step.
5. Most of the crypto-ransomware variants require administrative privilege to make changes in the system which are not allowed to regular users. No application should be allowed to gain full admin access; if it gains full administrative access and performs more write operation than regular threshold, it should be terminated. We observed during our empirical study more than 4000 writes and 800 reads from a single ransomware sample. Thus, write permissions and other administrative privileges for regular users should be limited.
6. There was a set of specific locations in Windows like .temp folder and tasks in C:\Windows\SysWow64 and C:Windows\System32, where ransomware tried to modify the contents. Thus, these locations in Windows should be placed under scrutiny to detect any malicious executable or malicious code.
7. There was a set of specific registry keys modified by ransomware. For example, a ransomware tends to alter SAFEBOOT option, to prevent booting the system in SAFE-MODE and avoid its deletion. A verification regarding alteration to SAFE-MODE by an executable should be made and if found, that executable should be terminated.
8. To prevent ransomware from spreading into a network and causing further damage, a system which is compromised by malware should be dis-connected immediately from the network. The victim should never pay the ransom, as it encourages the attacker to target more victims.

VIII. DISCUSSION

This section provides the post-experiment outcomes and related discussion. Indeed, crypto-ransomware has diverse impacts on the system registry and registry key values. A number of registries were modified and operated by the malware to ensure its persistence in the system. The ransomware deleted all backup and restoration points. There was a number of processes which were spawned during the attack process. Crypto-ransomware spreads to several legitimate processes of Windows to successfully invade the infected system. With the study of this malware, we were able to suggest a number of corresponding prevention recommendations as attackers always find a way to bypass defense mechanisms [15]. Unpatched vulnerabilities are the most common and easiest way for an attacker to deliver the payload, but a naive user is the best method to compromise the system. Crypto-ransomware disguises itself in any Windows folder-like "Program File" and "Temp", which should be constantly monitored. Thus, on the one hand, the user should not open any suspicious link. On the other hand, all vulnerabilities should be patched in order to prevent damage by crypto-ransomware.

IX. CONCLUSION

In this paper, we examined a set of crypto-ransomware in order to analyze the common behavior between them. We observed activities of the ransomware on a Windows system by performing a real-time attack in a virtual environment. Our results show different aspects of ransomware infecting the system. All the variants of crypto-ransomware affected the same registry values and deleted existing files. It was also observed that once the attack was completed, no encryption was performed on newly added files. Crypto-ransomware tends to perform more write operations when compared to a system's normal behavior. Based on our observations, we propose a set of recommendations to improve the current detection and prevention methods. Ransomware uses very strong encryption to attack, which is in general impossible to crack. Therefore, it is always recommended to protect the system in the first place. All variants of crypto-ransomware showed some typical signatures. In future work, we are proposing to use such signatures to enhance a new detection and prevention ransomware approach.

ACKNOWLEDGMENT

This work has been partly funded by a Public Safety Canada grant, and by the Computer Research Institute of Montréal (CRIM). We gratefully thank the Ministère de l'Économie, Science et Innovation du Québec (MESI) for its generous support.

REFERENCES

[1] F. Cuppens, N. Cuppens, J. Lanet, and L. Legay, "Risks and Security of Internet and Systems", 11th International Conference, CRiSIS 2016, Roscoff, France, pp. 5-7, 2017.

[2] N. Scaife, P. Traynor, and K. Butler, "Making Sense of the Ransomware Mess (and Planning a Sensible Path Forward)", IEEE Potentials, 36(6), pp. 28-31, 2017.

[3] M. Choudhary, P. Zavarsky, and D. Lindskog, "Experminetal Analysis of Ransomware on Windows and Android Platform: Evolution and Characterization", Procedia Computer Science, vol. 94, no. ISSN 1877- 0509, pp. 456-472, 2016.

[4] S. K. Pandey and B. M. Methre, "A Lifecycle Based Approach for Malware Analysis", Communication Systems and Network Technologies (CSNT), 2014 Fourth International Conference on. IEEE, 2014.

[5] N. Scaife, H. Carter, P. Traynor, and K. R. Butler, "CryptoLock (and Drop it): Stopping ransomware attack on user data", in Distributd Computing systems (ICDCS), 36th International Conference on. IEEE, 2016.

[6] A. Zahra and M.A. Shah, "IoT based ransomware growth rate evaluation and detection using command and control blacklisting", 23rd International Conference on Automation and Computing (ICAC), pp. 1-6, 2017.

[7] D. Maiorca, F. Mercaldo, G. Giacinto, C. A. Visaggio, and F. Martinelli, "R-PackDroid: API package-based characterization and detection of mobile ransomware", In Proceedings of the Symposium on Applied Computing, pp. 1718-1723, 2017.

[8] A. L. Young and M. Yung, "Cryptovirology: The birth, neglect, and explosion of ransomware", Communications of the ACM, 60 (7), pp. 24-26, 2017.

[9] C. Chung and N. Tan, "The Evolution of Ransomware From CryptoWall To CTB LOCKER", in Virus Bullentin Conference, Fortinet Techonlogy Inc., pp. 46-56, 2015.

[10] D. Bazdarevic and M. Dubell "Building ransomware for fun and profit academic research purposes", 2016.

[11] FireEye, "Ransomware Response Strategies From Identifying attack mechanisms to Detecting and blocking threats", FireEye.Inc, California, 2016.

[12] A. Ajjan and James Wyke, "The Current State of ransomware", A Sophos Labs Technical paper, pp. 1-61, 2016.

[13] A. Ali, "Ransomware: a research and a personal case study of dealing with this nasty malware", Issues in Informing Science and Information Technology, 14, pp. 87-99, 2017.

[14] A. Sanatinia and G. Noubir, "OnionBots: Subverting Privacy Infrastructure for Cyber Attacks", in 45th Annual IEEE\IFIP International Conference in Dependable System and Networks, pp. 69-80, 2015.

[15] E. Kirda, "UNVEIL: A large-scale, automated approach to detecting ransomware", In The IEEE 24th International Conference on Software Analysis, Evolution and Reengineering (SANER), pp. 1-2, 2017.

[16] X. Luo, and Q. Liao, "Awareness education as the key to ransomware prevention", Information Systems Security, 16 (4), pp. 195-202, 2007.

[17] C. Everett, "Ransomware: to pay or not to pay?", Computer Fraud & Security, (4), pp.8-12, 2017.

[18] R. Rivest, '"SA Security response to weaknesses in key scheduling algorithm of RC4". Technical note, RSA Data Security, Inc., pp.1-3, 2001.

[19] D. Gonzalez and T. Hayajneh, "Detection and prevention of crypto-ransomware", In Ubiquitous Computing, Electronics and Mobile Communication Conference (UEMCON), IEEE 8th Annual, pp. 472-478, 2017.

[20] N. Koblitz, "Elliptic curve cryptosystems". Mathematics of computation, 48(177), pp. 203-209, 1987.

Adaptive Security in Cloud and Edge Networks

New IoT Security Approach

Tewfiq El-Maliki, Nabil Abdennadher and Mohamed Nizar Bouchedakh
Information Technology department-hepia
University of Applied Sciences Western Switzerland
1202 Geneva - Switzerland
Email: {tewfiq.elmaliki, nabil.abdennadher, mohamed-nizar.bouchedakh}@hesge.ch

Abstract—Edge and cloud networks have emerged during the rapid evolution of networking in the last years, mainly as part of Internet of Things network. Security has become a key issue for any huge deployment in this network. Moreover, data reliability combined with performance is really a challenging task, particularly to maintain survivability of the network. This paper addresses this task using an Adaptation Security Framework, which is an efficient edge-cloud security deployment capable of trading-off between security and performance. It is based on an autonomic computing security looped system, which fine-tunes security means based on the monitoring of the context. An evaluation of the approach is undergoing in the context of smart city through a simulation tool and real-world large deployment.

Keywords **– Edge; Cloud; Framework; Autonomic; Security adaptation; Internet of Things (IoT).**

I. Introduction

Data Protection and trust are no longer just a compliance or security issue. They have become strategic topics since significant changes are introduced into the new European legislation. Indeed, it is highly challenging to maintain the overall security at the highest level due to the configuration complexity and the runtime changing context. The incoming edge computing as an adjacent network to the cloud creates many challenges, particularly in security field.

Accordingly, any concept that needs to cope with this new security challenge has to be based on overall performance aspects such as power consumption, this being a key issue in wireless networks, especially in sensor networks or the Internet of Things (IoT) [1]. It is imperative to address these problems from the earliest point of the system's design. All software development projects need a well-balanced amount of security awareness, right from the beginning [2].

In addition to the security challenge, data transfer in IoT is more susceptible to attack due to the nature of the edge nodes and the high error rate of wireless links. Therefore, the most crucial constraint in this network is reliability of any piece of information.

Trust mechanisms can solve these challenges. Indeed, they give a trust value about the behavior of an IoT device compared to standard behavior or similar IoT devices. By trust, we mean a particular level of a subjective opinion (Probability of a value - temperature, humidity, image etc. - to be accurate) with which an edge device will perform a particular action for many applications.

There is a rapidly growing literature on the theory and applications of trust systems. General surveys could be found easily and we suggest the survey of Josang [3], which is a reference in this field.

Moreover, IoT data sensing may be affected by deterioration of the hardware and environmental perturbations. However, we deploy multiple space located homogeneous sensors to provide redundant information to fix the uncertainty of sensing. This approach gives flexibility and cost-effectiveness to the deployment of IoT devices and deals with fault tolerance, random errors as well as the drift of the sensitivity or accuracy of the measurements of the IoT devices overtime [4]. Thereby, we do not need any heavy full security process to trust a single value obtained from an IoT device, as long as we have a lot of similar value extracted from cheap IoT devices spread over the entire environment. A spatio-temporal correlation could be used to rate the relevance of any value of a device to his neighbors' values.

Thanks to trust, we could build a solid general trust system to rate the accuracy, sensitivity and quality of wireless connection of any IoT device related to the provided data over time. Many trust models for wireless environment have been proposed, such one is described in [5] and the trust model for data described in [6].

In general, many applications can not operate under significant packet loss. Thus, reliability is one of the important criteria to evaluate the quality of wireless IoT networks. Thereof, the concept that must cope with this new security challenge has to be based on dynamic adaptation security system to satisfy an overall performance such as network reliability, being a key issue especially in sensor networks. We have already proposed a generic security adaptation framework as a compelling solution for such problems [7]. In this article, we will apply it to the IoT network by dividing our Security Adaptation Framework (ASF) into edge security part and cloud security part. The two parts will collaborate to optimize global security.

In this paper, we use security in a general sense including availability, reliability and survivability.

The rest of the paper is structured as follows. In Section 2, we give the motivation of our work. Section 3 introduces ASF for IoT and explains its components and functionalities.

Section 4 concludes our paper and sketches the future work for validation and consolidation.

II. Motivation for our Framework

Edge or fog network aims to develop a new concept in networking, which stands on new context-aware sensors capabilities [8]. Sending and processing huge amounts of data to the cloud will not be "reasonable" due to latency and bandwidth limitation.

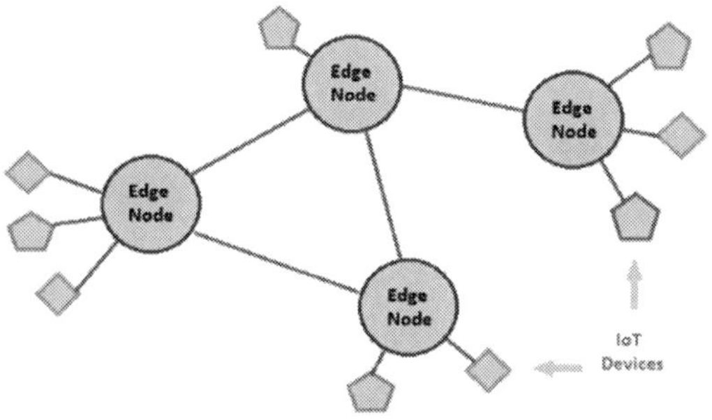

Figure 1. Edge node in IoT network

Edge computing could be the alternative. It will involve IoT connected devices capabilities in order to proceed locally rather than sending data to the cloud. Smart devices might be able to provide users' services and alleviate some latency issues. In figure 1, we see a typical edge network. The tendency is to use edge network as a distributed network. Edge computing covers a wide range of technologies including wireless sensor networks, mobile data acquisition, mobile signature analysis, cooperative distributed peer-to-peer ad-hoc networking and processing known as local cloud/fog computing and grid/mesh computing. It uses distributed data storage and retrieval system, autonomic self-healing networks, virtual cloudlets, remote cloud services, augmented reality, and more.

The approach is based on the principle of divide and conquer and it will guarantee the scalability by dividing the IoT universe into interconnected domains where a domain is associated to an edge node. This creates a sort of hierarchy that helps with the addressing and localization problems especially in dynamic networks with mobile devices.

The increasing complexity of communication in IoT applications makes the conventional static security almost obsolete, such as public key infrastructure. New mechanisms need to be set up in order to address this problem. One of the alternatives consists in using autonomic system techniques [9] to design adaptive security policy tailored to IoT applications.

Security in sensor networks [10] is complicated by the constrained capabilities of sensor node hardware and the properties of the deployment. Individual sensor nodes in our case have inherent limitations in resources, which makes the design of security procedures more complicated. Each of these limitations is due in part to the two greatest constraints: limited energy and physical size.

Other security issues include security-energy assessment, data assurance, survivability, trust, end to end security, security support for data centric sensor networks and node compromise distribution. Due to a sensor network's special characteristics, it is very important to study areas such as: battery limitation, high failure probability nodes, easily compromised nodes, unreliable transmission media, etc. Mobility greatly exacerbates the problem. A lack of synergy between the cloud and edge security mechanisms is also noticed. Nowadays, there have been only a few approaches available, and more studies are needed in these areas [11]. On the other hand, trust is a good path to explore because it could give better results for some specific cases.

The best way to overcome these constraints is to implement a framework capable of adapting security to the "context" based on the ideas similar to those described in [12] and consequently having an overall security control. This idea is inspired by the concept of autonomic computing and an efficient Security Adaptation framework called SARM [7]. In this project, our new framework is called ASF (Figure 2).

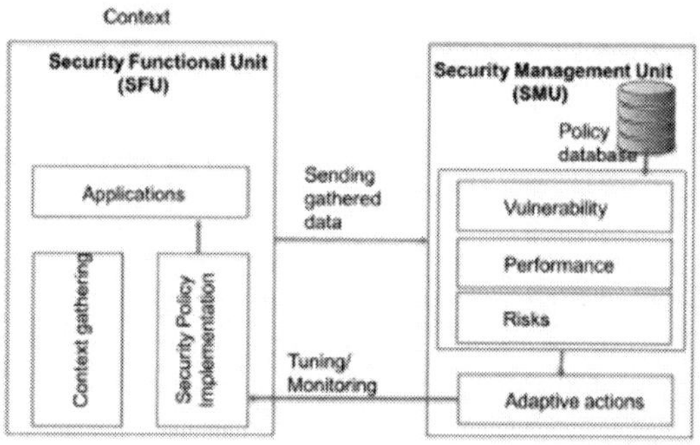

Figure 2. High level ASF approach.

The idea behind ASF is to adapt the security policy according to the context of the application. A security functional unit implements and executes the security policy, it gathers data related to the context and sends them to a security management unit. The security management unit can decide to update the security means in order to react to the new context.

III. ASF Description

A. ASF

We would like with ASF to fine-tune security means as best as possible taking into account the risk of the current application environment and the performance of the system especially regarding the optimization of its energy consumption. Thereby, our system differs from others by its [7]:

a) Autonomic computing security looped system

b) Dynamic and evolving security mechanisms related to context-monitoring

c) Explicit energy consumption management

The concept of isolating various functions and restricting their access to specific systems can also be applied to security in wireless environment integrated in the mobile operating system itself. The best way to overcome the nonrealistic constraint of implementing the framework in each communication program is to integrate it in the kernel and consequently having an overall security control. Thus, all communication programs go through ASF at some stage in order to gain access to communication resources.

Information about ASF high-level components can be found in [5].

B. *ASF for IoT*

Having a centrally distributed (respectively cloud-edge) system helps deploy distributed IoT applications with central components deployed on cloud level and distributed components deployed on edge nodes.

For these reasons, we propose an autonomous and adaptive security system with two levels/scopes:

The first level consists of a "Local ASF" that manages security means locally on the edge node by using inputs coming from the local IoT environment (local IoT devices, gateways, etc). The role of the local ASF is to adapt the security means on the edge node to the local context changes with respect to a local security policy that implements general rules (e.g., energy saving, performance) and users' preferences.

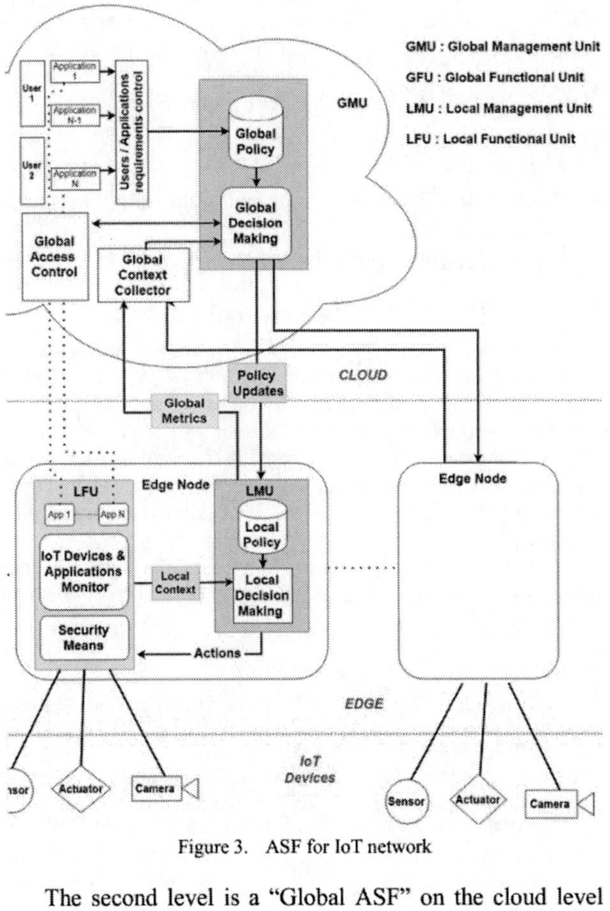

Figure 3. ASF for IoT network

The second level is a "Global ASF" on the cloud level that has a global view of the overall system (edge nodes, IoT devices and gateways). The global ASF's role is (1) to control deployments of distributed application components on the edge nodes, (2) to update the local ASF policy with security updates or with new user's preferences, (3) to adapt security means on the edge network level based on the global context gathered from different edge nodes and based on the global security policy.

Figure 3 represents with details the deployment of ASF for IoT network. It shows the separation cloud-edge and local-global units

This architecture guarantees a loose cooperation between local "edge" ASF and global "cloud" ASF. In fact, the global ASF is an enabler that helps the local ASF perform better but a local ASF could work just fine by itself. So, in case of a connection failure between the cloud and the edge node, as its name implies, a local ASF can run perfectly.

A promising approach is to use a trust and reputation based system to assess trustworthiness of IoT devices or edge devices. Our proposed solution uses trust estimation of IoT devices, on the edge nodes level, as one of the security means of the local ASF. We also use trust estimation of the edge nodes, on the cloud level, based on the trust and the reputation. This later concept (reputation) is an indicator that assesses a nodes trustworthiness based on the indirect trust a.k.a the recommendations of other nodes of the network. Reputation is usable on the global ASF's level thanks to the interaction between edge nodes and the global view of the system.

C. *Trust for IoT*

When the IoT application is not critical and does not require individual authentication of the IoT devices, we can replace the "stringent" authentication/encryption method by a heuristic estimation of the "trust" we can assign to IoT devices. This method overcomes the limitation of the traditional security mechanism. In many cases, trust management is the key to building trustworthy and reliable IoT networks.

Trust evaluates the overall behavior of IoT devices. It is often calculated as follows:

a) receive data from the IoT device,

b) use a reference model (previously set-up) to "extract" information modeling the consistency of the received data,

c) use this information to calculate the trust of the IoT device.

The trust value assigned to a peace of data (received from a given IoT device) is used to make necessary "arrangements": isolate the IoT device, fix the problem, etc.

Trust of an IoT device (or the data coming from a given IoT device) can be represented by a function of several parameters, which are related to:

a) the connection with the edge device: Example: in a wireless connection, one of the parameters is the Packet Error Rate (PER),

b) the correlations of the IoT device with "temporal" factors: Example: temperature is lower during the night and higher during the day, the correlations of IoT devices with "spatial" factors: two neighbor sensors should provide similar measures.

Each of these parameters is weighted by a coefficient, which reflects its relevance. Thereby, the trust of a given device is represented by a function:

$$\text{TrustFunct(IoT-device)} = \alpha_0 * \pi_0 + ... + \alpha i * \pi i \quad (1)$$

where α_i are the coefficients and π_i are the parameters.

The coefficients may vary from one IoT application to another. This means that an IoT device has different values of trust for different IoT applications. Indeed, trust is a subjective value and each application has its own rating value depending on the end user security policy. Hence, TrustFunct should be written as follow:

$$\text{TrustFunct(IoT-device,IoT-App)} = \alpha_0 * \pi_0 + ... + \alpha i * \pi i \quad (2)$$

In equation (2), coefficients αi are related to the IoT application.

IoT devices having the same "features" (for example, measuring the same thing: temperature, humidity, pressure, etc.) must use the same Trust function for the same IoT application.

The objective of the "trust for data" mechanism is to develop a trust management system and deploy it on the cloud/edge device. This trust management system must set up the coefficients of the trust function (TrustFunct) for each IoT device. These coefficients are calculated according to a simplified version of the method presented in [6].

For each data value received from an IoT device, deduce the estimated values of the different parameters composing the Trust function (πi). These estimations are often based on machine learning methods and then calculate the trust value of the IoT device using (2).

This subsection introduces trust for data in a simplified way. In several research and industrial projects, trust computing is more complicated than presented here: it is done between edge devices and the cloud: machine learning (ML) models are generated by the cloud and sent to the edge devices. The edge devices receive data from the IoT devices, calculate the parameters of the trust function by using the ML models and send feedback to the cloud, which corrects the ML models and sends them back to the edge devices. As an illustration of this approach, the reader can view the Microsoft Azure solution [13].

D. *Validation Application Domain: Smart City*

To validate the model, we will apply an adapted version of ASF to the application domain of IoT – Smart City. In this domain, the trust value of IoT devices will be based on the solution described in the last subsection. The trust function (2) will be mainly based on four common parameters, accuracy, sensitivity, response time and packet error rate. According to the type of the IoT device, other specific parameters could be considered.

The common definitions of the four parameters listed in (2) will be:

Accuracy : accuracy of a sensor is the maximum difference existing between the actual value and the value received from the sensor,

Sensitivity: sensibility of a sensor is the minimum input of a physical parameter that creates a detectable output change,

Response time: the response time is the time required for a sensor output to change from its previous state to a final settled value,

PER: PER is the number of incorrectly received data packets divided by the total number of received packets. PER evaluates the quality of the transmission channel over time. It is used for evaluating the reliability of the transmission channel. This last parameter is extracted directly from the data link layer.

To calculate the three first parameters, we need two inputs:

a) data received from the IoT device and, "estimation" of the real value. This estimation is deduced from a predictive model based on machine learning,

b) machine Learning models runs on the edge devices. They are generated and updated in the cloud.

The trust (trust function) is calculated in the edge devices. It can be transferred to the cloud in order to have a global overview of the trust at the scale of the entire IoT platform.

Therefore, we would like to achieve global objectives:

a) keeping an appropriate level of security at edge level depending on the context ;

b) whilst maximizing the overall data reliability at the cloud level;

c) and controling the overall security .

IV. CONCLUSION AND FUTURE WORK

We have proposed a Security Adaptation Framework for IoT based on concomitant combination of edge and cloud ASF repartition. It uses an Autonomic Computing Security pattern to support both context monitor and behavior control. This paper explains the trust approach that will be used based on tempo-spatial correlation between sensors using machine learning. The validation will be in a context of smart city project.

Other strategies that could automatically optimize the trade-off between overall security and data trust will be explored.

REFERENCES

[1] F. Hamad, L. Smalov, and A. James, "Energy-aware Security in M-Commerce and the Internet of Things", IETE. 26: pp. 357-362, 2009.

[2] J. Chen, C. Hu, and H. Zeng, "A Novel Model for Evaluating Optimal Parameters of Security and Quality of Service" - Journal of Computers, VOL. 5, NO. 6, pp. 973-978, 2010.

[3] A. Josang, R. Ismail, and C. Boyd, "A Survey of Trust and Reputation Systems for Online Service Provision", Decision Support Systems, 43(2), pp. 618-644, 2007.

[4] E.Asmare and J. McCann, "Lightweight Sensing Uncertainty Metric – Incorporating Accuracy and Trust", IEEE Sensors Journal, pp. 4264 – 4272, 2014.

[5] T. El-Maliki, "Security Adaptation in Highly Dynamic Wireless Networks", Ph.D. thesis, 2014.

[6] R. Gwadera, M. Riahi, and K. Aberer "Pattern-wise trust assessment of sensor data", 15th IEEE International Conference on Mobile Data Management IEEE MDM 2014.

[7] T. El Maliki and J-M Seigneur "Security Adaptation Based on Autonomic and Trust Systems for Ubiquitous mobile network and Green IT", Ubicomm 2013.

[8] K. Bierzynski, A. Escobar and M. Eberl, "Cloud, fog and edge: Cooperation for the future?", Second International Conference on Fog and Mobile Edge Computing (FMEC), 2017.

[9] M. Parashar and S. Hariri, "Autonomic Computing: An overview", vol 3566, Springer, Berlin, Heidelberg 2005.

[10] T. El-Maliki and J.-M. Seigneur, "Security Adaptation Based on Autonomic and Trust Systems for Ubiquitous mobile network and Green", The Seventh International Conference on Mobile Ubiquitous Computing, Systems, Services and Technologies, Portugal, UBICOMM, 2013.

[11] R. Roman, J. Lopez and M. Mambo, "Mobile edge computing, Fog et al.: A survey and analysis of security threats and challenges", Future Generation Computer Systems, vol. 78, pp. 680-698, 2018.

[12] B. Badrinath, A. Fox, L Kleonrock, G. Popek, and M. Satyanarayanan, "A conceptual Framework for Network and Client Adaptation", Mobile Networks and applications, v.5 n.4, Dec. 2000, pp. 221-231, 2000.

[13] https://azure.microsoft.com/en-us/services/machine-learning-studio/ [accessed April 2018]

Knowledge-driven Vaccine Systems Engineering

Leonard Petnga
Department of Industrial and Systems Engineering
University of Alabama in Huntsville
Huntsville, AL 35899, USA
Email: leonard.petnga@uah.edu

Surangi Jayawardena
Department of Chemistry
University of Alabama in Huntsville
Huntsville, AL 35899, USA
Email: surangi.jayawardena@uah.edu

Abstract—**Current vaccine development approaches are ineffective in capturing, representing and reconciling domains and disciplines knowledge and viewpoints across the vaccine development life cycle. As a result, vaccine development is a long, complex, and costly process that often results (when it succeeds) in vaccines whose potency is hard to predict and efficacy expensive to preserve. State-of-the-art vaccine development approaches fail to (1) integrate the multiplicity of stakeholders perspectives across the Vaccine Development Life Cycle (VDLC), (2) bridge the knowledge gap between multiple disciplines, and (3) formally evaluate stochastic system behaviors of biological systems in a seamless manner. This paper introduces a novel semantically-enabled framework for knowledge and behavior specification, modeling and processing in vaccine systems engineering. Data and semantic models of domains supported by sound theories and tightly coupled with Markov Chain models of biological systems are the cornerstone of our solution. Near future work includes optimal vaccine matrix design and experimental vaccine preservation systems. Looking ahead, the capabilities of the framework – demonstrated in a vaccine preservation study – will enable more effective, cheaper and faster time-to-market vaccines.**

Keywords-Vaccine; Systems Engineering; Semantic; Ontology; Markov Chain.

I. Introduction

A. Problem statement

Vaccination is a cornerstone of today's modern human being health of all ages, preventing potentially fatal and life crippling diseases. Successful vaccines – such as the one for smallpox – have rid the world of a severely contagious and potentially fatal disease. The core component of the vaccine – the vaccine antigen – is formulated and designed to be administered as an oral vaccine or injected subcutaneously. Successful vaccines provide lifelong immunity and protection of the host from contracting diseases caused by corresponding pathogens.

The effectiveness of the immunization is contingent upon multiple factors, including the nature and behavior of the pathogen, the vaccine and its development life cycle, and the host physiology. The difficulty in engineering, developing, manufacturing and delivering highly effective vaccines is complicated by its variant nature, a characteristic inherent to all biological systems [1]. In rare occasions, host physiology coupled with genetic factors and environmental conditions can adversely affect the vaccination outcome through immunosuppression or anaphylaxis (severe reactions). Stakeholders involved in the Vaccine Development Life Cycle (VDLC) – see Figure 1 – view the vaccine through significantly different lens, which makes elicitation of design requirements very difficult. For instance, researchers (e.g., Stage 1 of VDLC) are more interested in the immunological processes at the molecular level (antigen), while clinicians (e.g., Stage 7) are looking for faster, more effective, accurate and less invasive delivery tools and mechanisms. Moreover, the knowledge disconnect between the disciplines involved – biology, chemistry, engineering, manufacturing, legal, regulatory and healthcare – makes vaccine development a very convoluted process [1].

The compounding effect of these issues contributes to today's situation where vaccines (1) are available for only 10% of known pathogens harmful to human, (2) cost hundreds of millions of dollars to develop and 8 to 10 years from research to market with high failure rates, (3) have short shelf life span i.e., a year or less and, (4) require costly and stringent storage and handling conditions [2][3]. Moreover, fast genetic mutations of pathogens of deadly ailments (e.g., HIV-1) and environment factors have been enabling them to outsmart researchers for years, making vaccine development for those diseases an uphill battle. The stakes are even higher when we consider social and cultural resistances to immunization. Concerns about (and risks of) childhood autism, anaphylaxis, disabilities, contraction of vaccine associated diseases (live vaccines) and religious beliefs are among the most common arguments against vaccination [4].

Addressing these challenges requires vaccine design and development approaches that enable stakeholders along the VDLC to answer both domain specific and cross-domain questions quickly, accurately and cheaply in the context of highly stochastic and complex biological dynamics. Leading research efforts in rational design of vaccines are piecewise and fail to address critical methodological and knowledge gaps [5]. Built upon the ability of the systems engineering discipline to bridge the gap between – and integrate – disciplines and architect systems at various levels of abstractions, the introduction of a model based knowledge-driven framework for vaccine development life cycle is a significant step forward. The three pillars of this work are that (1) formal methods must drive and support the development of models, (2) the latter must properly capture the depth and breadth of stochastic behaviors of biological systems and, (3) models must be reusable, customizable and

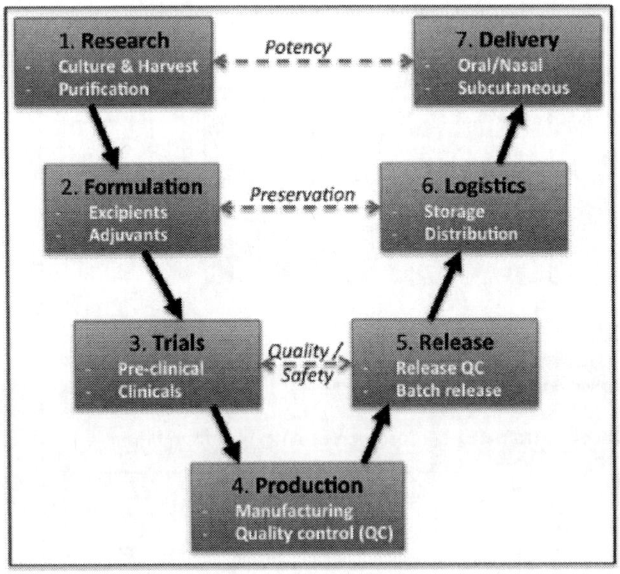

Figure 1. "Vee" model of the Vaccine Development Life Cycle (VDLC)

integrated at will for the purpose of the analysis at hand. State-of-the-art vaccine development approaches are not capable of such cross-discipline and cross-domain modeling and coverage of the life cycle [2][3][5].

B. Project Scope and Objectives

In order to address these limitations, we aim to develop the foundational semantic infrastructure for knowledge and behavior specification, modeling and processing across the full spectrum of the VDLC. The integration of biological system dynamic models and discipline and stakeholder knowledge models will enable the emergence of novel architectures whose instantiation and execution can be checked against the requirements of a given application or analysis. For instance, a researcher – in Stage 2 of Figure 1 – can make use of the integrated knowledge models of the formulation matrix and the stochastic model of the vaccine antigen to analyze the performance of the selected matrix and validate the results against experimental outcomes and incrementally refine the models accordingly. Elements of the study and its results can be propagated to the healthcare administrator (at Stage 6) to ensure proper handling of the vaccine in order to preserve its effectiveness while in storage and transit. Here, the creation and integration of knowledge and stochastic models of both the formulated vaccine and the environment is necessary. The healthcare professional in Stage 7 concerned with patient prognostic and response to the vaccine will need stochastic models of their physiology coupled to the one of the formulated vaccine, integrated with the knowledge model of the delivery protocol.

A successful implementation of this framework in full will make these scenarios and more complex ones a reality in the day-to-day work of stakeholders across the VDLC. More importantly, it will enable progress toward the development of an integrated, evolving *"vaccine digital twin"* whose sound mathematical foundations provide confidence in analyses, speed up decision making (thus, time-to-market) and help manage complexity more effectively.

Section II provides a brief review of vaccine types, mechanisms and development processes in the context of systems engineering. Section III introduces the foundations of the vaccine development semantic framework and describes its architecture. In Section IV, we briefly highlight two research topics currently under investigation that make use of, or reinforce the capabilities of the semantic framework. A simple vaccine preservation study example is presented in Section V. We conclude this work in Section VI.

II. VACCINE SYSTEMS ENGINEERING

A. Vaccines: Types and Development Challenges

Vaccines play a critical role in combating infectious disease and improving overall quality of living. There are several different types of vaccines: *live attenuated* vaccines (e.g., oral polio vaccine), *inactivated* vaccines (e.g., injectable polio vaccine), *subunit* vaccines, *toxoid* vaccines, *conjugate* vaccines, *DNA* vaccines (e.g., Hepatitis B) and *recombinant viral vectors* vaccines. The differences between the types of vaccines stem from the structure and properties of their core-component, i.e., the antigen. A vaccine achieves immunity through a complex process in the body and protects the host by inducing immune mechanisms capable of rapidly controlling replicating pathogens or inactivating their toxic components. One such mechanism is raising antibodies against the vaccine antigen.

The development of vaccines of any type is a complex, expensive and high-risk undertaking, as many candidates fail in pre-clinical studies (Stage 3 of VDLC). The key to success here lies in the vaccine's ability to induce an effective and sustained immune response, have minimal side effects, and be produced cost-effectively at large scale. Because of the complex nature of vaccine manufacturing, it is important to be able to understand, control and/or predict the factors that impact the efficacy, stability and safety of the vaccine along its process-engineering pathway.

B. Systems Engineering of Vaccines

The vaccine development life cycle can be represented similarly to the well known systems engineering "Vee" model, as shown in Figure 1. The first stage of vaccine development involves the selection of a candidate vaccine (exploratory stage) from a fundamental research laboratory and its testing using animal models (pre-clinical stage), followed by the development of small case scale material and formulation to make material for phases I, II and III studies (clinical development). Phase I includes safety tests among 10-100 human subjects to evaluate clinical responses. Then, phase II looks at the evaluation of immune responses in 100-3,000 subjects. Finally, in phase III, large scale studies are conducted to test vaccine efficacy and tolerance. Only vaccines that successfully pass trials are eventually mass produced. On the right side of the model, the vaccine is thoroughly tested before its release, then distributed in lots, and finally administered to the host. Three cross-cutting concerns between stages are identified: quality/safety, preservation and potency. However, unlike traditional systems engineering "Vee" models, the concerns are non-binding and there are no rigorous feedback mechanisms between successive stages, nor formal requirements flow down and traceability process.

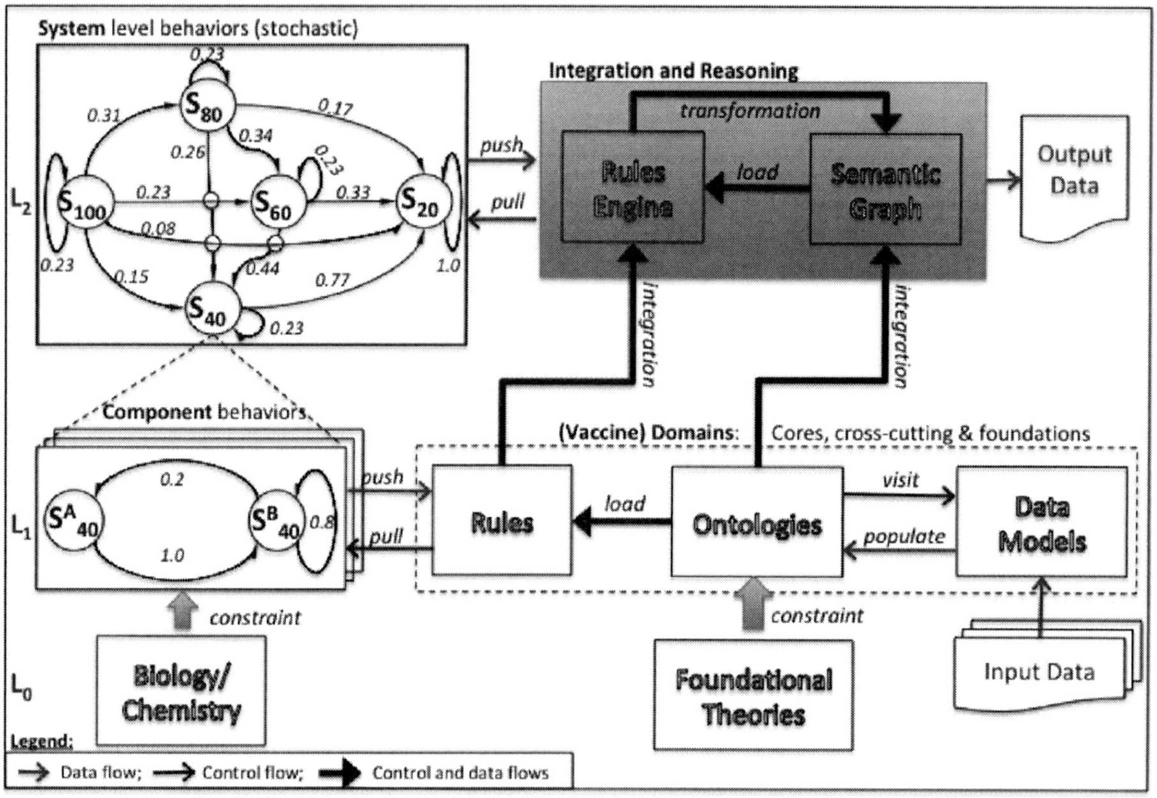

Figure 2. Simplified architecture of the framework

III. Semantic Framework for Vaccine Development Life Cycle

The development of semantic architectures for VDLC is complicated by the multiplicity of stakeholders' perspectives across the VDLC, the need to bridge the knowledge gap between multiple disciplines, and formally evaluate stochastic system behaviors of biological systems. We report in this section on a novel semantic-driven framework that addresses these challenges through a careful investigation, selection and integration of technologies, theories and models from relevant disciplines, domains and types.

A. *Logic-based Semantics and Semantic Web Technologies*

In order for core vaccine knowledge to be integrated, shared and reused across the various stages of the life cycle depicted in Figure 1, it must (1) be captured, represented in a clear, unambiguous way with respect to the associated domain and the context of use and, (2) lend itself to automated processing and reasoning by machines. Thus, data must be enriched by sound semantics to ensure accuracy of facts and inferencing.

Thanks to their sound mathematical foundations and decidability as fragment of first order logics, Description Logics (DL) formalisms have been shown effective in tackling the first part of this challenge [6]. A summary of description logic concepts constructors can be found in [7]. DLs provide the mathematical foundations on top of which machine and human readable ontological languages, such as the web ontology language (OWL) can be built in a systematic way. They enable the creation of ontologies, which are engineering artifacts that provide explicit specifications of the intended meaning of a vocabulary used to describe a given domain. Ontological models provide semantic meanings that enrich the way models can be branched and integrated across domains of knowledge automatically. These capabilities are critical to this work given the strong need to understand intricate relationships spanning multiple domains and components and their ultimate affects on the vaccine performance. In [8], we have identified and described the necessary extensions to the basic DL, leading to $\mathcal{SHOIN}$ and $\mathcal{SROIQ}$ DLs as appropriate logic-based formalisms for semantic framework like the one we are introducing in this work. OWL2 DL is computationally decidable and will support ontologies representations in our framework.

Semantic web technologies integrated with reasoner through Application Programming Interfaces (e.g., Jena) provide a way forward in addressing the second part of the above-mentioned challenge [8]. Together, the eXtensible Markup Language (XML), the Resource Description Framework (RDF) and OWL as hierarchical layers of the semantic web technology stack, allow for the implementation of reasoning that can prove whether or not assertions in the knowledge base are true or false in almost real-time (decidability). Thus, semantic web technologies are great enablers of automated processing and reasoning over sparse, across-domain information. In the context of VDLC, they will organize and merge the sources for answering biological and engineering questions using corresponding semantic models (ontologies, rules and computation extensions).

B. Mathematical Modeling of Systems Biology

The effective capture and representation of the behavior of the biological systems (e.g., vaccine antigen, host physiology) across the VDLC necessitates models that accurately capture the essence of unfolding biological (and underlining) chemical processes at various level of abstractions. Such models must allow the simulation of the system behavior over time and predict changes caused by interactions with other systems and the environment. Modeling schemes of biological phenomenons and systems emphasize various aspects such as body metabolism, genetic networks, neuronal systems or processes (e.g., intracellular processes). These models have been shown appropriate for cellular level analyses and studies but they are ineffective in capturing biological phenomenons that occur at higher levels of abstractions (e.g., tissue, organs)[9]. Thus, we will choose Markov models which have been demonstrated effective in modeling and predicting the behavior of highly stochastic biological [10] and biomedical systems [11]. Plus, they are not domain specific and they lend themselves well to integration through segmentation mechanism to domain specific models. *Markov chain (MC)* – see top left corner of Figure 2 – states (S_i), in our framework, represent a valid biological or chemical state with arrows between states annotated with their probability of propagation. Feedback between states and steady-states are allowed with the constraint that all propagation probabilities at each state must sum to one (1). *Hidden Markov models* extend Markov chain models and are developed from observed system performance (e.g., lab experiments). The resulting model is then used to further the analysis of the system and predict future behavior.

C. Simplified System Architecture

The proposed knowledge-driven framework shown in Figure 2 makes use of logic-based semantics emulated by semantic web technologies and MC to provide rigorous formalisms to models across the VDLC. It is modular and its building blocks are chosen and integrated depending on the needs and requirements of a given application. The architecture is organized into three layers as follows.

Foundation Layer (L_0). The mathematical foundations needed by architectural models reside here. Foundation theories (for known cross-cutting domains such as time, physical quantities, communication, etc.) are distinguished from biological and chemistry laws or well-accepted domain standards (e.g., CDC Standard for Adult Immunization Practice). One such theory is Allen Temporal Interval Calculus (ATIC), which has been shown effective in supporting formal description and reasoning in the temporal domain [8].

Domain Knowledge Layer (L_1). The VDLC knowledge is organized into three groups: core domains (e.g., vaccine antigen, host), cross-cutting domains (e.g., storage condition, vaccine schedule) and foundation domains (e.g., time, physical quantity). Each domain knowledge is encoded in the form of a "semantic block" made of (1) an ontology, (2) set of rules, and (3) interfaces that enable communication between semantic blocks and linking with computation platforms and Markov models of system biology via customized builtin functions. Data models provide the templates for input data to be processed by the semantic block. DLs provide the formalisms needed by core domains knowledge while theories such as the ATIC will constrain models of some cross-cutting domains (e.g., vaccine schedule). Requirements are captured as a cross-cutting domain that makes use of foundation knowledge to formally encode and process input textual requirements.

Integration Layer (L_2). Bridging the knowledge gap between disciplines in the framework requires (1) the integration of domain specific knowledge at level L_1 on both the semantic and stochastic behavior sides, and (2) linking them to emulate system level behavior for the application under consideration. The resulting (system) semantic graph is transformed as rules – integrated to stochastic models of the system behavior – are fired. It can also act as semantic controller as it could encode defined system metrics whose instances could be checked against system requirements (as constraints). We will trust the Whistle scripting environment [12] with the controlled and systematic assembly of the models, as well as simulation and output generation.

IV. Work in Progress

The architecture introduced and briefly described in Section III is generic and high level enough to be customized for various applications and challenges throughout the VDLC. We are working toward its use and adaptation to tackle two important challenges in the VDLC: determining and characterizing the best formulation mix for a vaccine and designing experimental vaccine preservation systems.

A. Topic 1: Vaccine Formulation Design

The challenge of retaining potency (or efficacy) of the vaccine until it is administered remains an open challenge for researchers [13][14]. The potency of the vaccine has to be preserved throughout the VDLC from its formulation (Stage 2 of VDLC) to the administration (Stage 7) through manufacturing (Stage 4) and subsequent steps. The design of the best vaccine matrix (i.e., the formulate) able to stabilize, preserve and improve host immune response is a multi-domain, multi-disciplinary and complex integration problem for which the architecture developed in this work can help address. For each vaccine, design of experiments will help narrow down the most effective excipients (stabilizers and preservatives) and adjuvants from a list of over 370 substances that are Generally Recognized As Safe (GRAS) [15]. Then, both knowledge and stochastic models of selected substances will be integrated in the framework along with the ones of the vaccine and the pathogen. The response will be traded across multiple objectives (e.g., potency, infectivity), conditions (e.g., temperature, moisture) and configurations of the mixture.

B. Topic 2: Experimental Vaccine Preservation Systems

Under the current state-of-the-art of vaccine technologies, the most effective matrix cannot preserve it from becoming subpotent due to inappropriate and suboptimal storage, handling and transportation, especially under challenging infrastructural, economical and environmental conditions [16][17]. This project will build from the results from Topic 1 and previous related work in biomedical devices [11] to analyze, develop and verify prototype adaptive platform-based containers for vaccines handling and storage. The focus will be on enabling and demonstrating system resilience to frequent changes in environmental conditions such as the ones currently observed along the vaccine supply chain [17]. Another interest of the project will be to understand mechanisms through which decisions (e.g., vaccine type, matrix elements) early in the VDLC ultimately constraint and affect preservation platforms (to be) used in vaccine supply chain downstream. Thus, we plan to extend the capability of the framework introduced in this work by integrating it with graph-based database platforms [18].

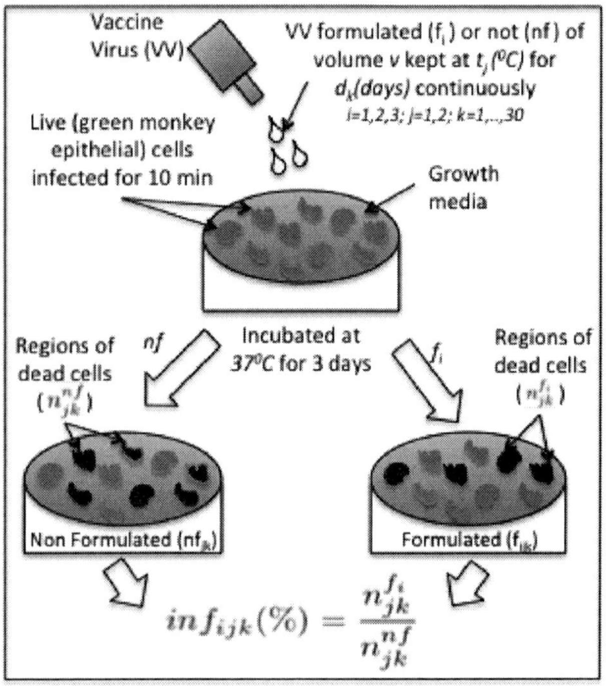

Figure 3. Schematics of the OPV preservation experiment

V. Prototype: Vaccine Preservation Study

A. Experiment Set Up and Methodology

We illustrate the basic implementation and use of our framework in a simplified Oral Polio Vaccine (OPV) formulation study for which the corresponding experiment is pictured in Figure 3. The study seeks to evaluate how well given formulations (f_i) preserve the effectiveness of the OPV (live attenuated) under stringent preservation conditions (temperature) such as the ones observed in Sub Saharan Africa. In a simplified experimental design, a volume v of a formulated OPV (vaccine antigen virus, VV) kept at temperature t_j during d_k days, is administered to n numbers of host cells (live, green monkey epithelial cells). The host cells are infected with the virus for 10 mins, and the excess vaccine removed. A layer of agarose gel is placed on top of the host cells and the cells are incubated at 37^0C for 3 days. Then, the gel is removed and the host cells is stained. Finally, dead regions of the cells or plaques $n_{jk}^{f_i}$ are counted. The same experiment is repeated for all the formulations and for the non-formulated VV and n_{jk}^{nf} is recorded. The infectivity – i.e., how well the vaccine was preserved by a given formulation f_i– is computed as follows.

$$inf_{ijk}(\%) = \frac{n_{jk}^{f_i}}{n_{jk}^{nf}} \tag{1}$$

The framework represents the actual experiment through the capture and modeling of core elements relevant to the study. Simplified ontologies and rules for the biology domain (cell, vaccine and pathogen) and the experiment domain (parameters, set up) are created and integrated as described in Section III. The behavior of the VV is modeled using instances of the simple MC pictured on the top left corner of Figure 2. The states S_p ($p \in P = \{20, 40, 60, 80, 100\}$) represent the virulence of the vaccine, which can only degrade from $p = 100\%$ to $p = 20\%$ in this simplified prototype. The transition probabilities depend on the experimental setup and they are driven by a "degradation factor" k_{ijk}^{tf} which characterizes the ability of the system to maintain itself in a state S_p under the given experimental setup. It's defined as follows.

$$k_{ijk}^{tf} = \left[\frac{T_{Max} - t_j}{T_{Max} t_j (100 - C_{f_i})}\right]^{\frac{d_k}{d_{Max}}} \tag{2}$$

where T_{max} is the maximum allowable exposure temperature for the experiment and $C_{f_i} \in (0, 100)$ is a coefficient characterizing the "degradation resistance" of a given formulation. One such formulation for the OPV can comprise antibiotics Neomycin and Kanamycin as preservatives and $MgCl_2$ as stabilizer. As indicated in research Topic 2, design of experiments is a way forward to narrow down the list of candidate formulations. The transitions between states (S_p) are computed as follows.

$$a_{ijk}^{tf}|_{p,q} = (1 - \Delta_{ijk}^{tf}|_{p,q}) k_a k_{ijk}^{tf} \tag{3}$$

where $\Delta_{ijk}^{tf}|_{p,q}$ is the gap of virulence between a state of virulence p and one of virulence $q < p$ in P and $k_a > 0$ is a balancing coefficient allowing the probabilities to sum to 1 as per Markov Chains modeling rules. We note that $a_{ijk}^{tf}|_{20,20} = 1$ to capture the fact that any decrease of the virulence of the VV below 20% is beyond the sensitivity level of our analysis thus, not relevant. This results into a full MC model driving the generation of the values of $n_{jk}^{f_i}$ and n_{jk}^{nf} that we use to calculate the infectivity of the VV when mixed with the cell. The MC is implemented as a built-in function linked to the rule that determines the value of the infectivity based on the experiment setup. Given the small size of our prototype input/output data, there is no need to implement full data models for this instance of the framework.

B. Results

For the prototype simulation, we select three formulations f_i with low ($C_{f_1} = 5$), medium ($C_{f_2} = 50$) and high ($C_{f_3} = 95$) degradation resistance. Also, we assume the VV samples are conserved at ambient ($t_1 = 25^0C$) and body ($t_2 = 37^0C$) temperatures respectively, over selected periods of duration $d_k \in (1, .., 30)$ days. In order to assess the performance of our formulations, we refer to the acceptable infectivity threshold for administration of oral polio vaccine, which is $inf_{ijk} = 40\%$ [19]. The latter is known as the "infectivity threshold" below which the formulation is considered ineffective to ensure full potency of the vaccine. Figure 4 shows the result of the simulation for t_1 with $T_{Max} = 40^0C$. The formulations outperform each other as their C_f is higher up to the 2/3 of the maximum exposure time around $d = 20$ days, right before the potency baseline is crossed (around $d_b = 21$ days for all). After that, there seems to be no additional benefit in higher C_f. Similar results (not shown) are observed for $t_2 = 37^0C$. This suggests that this vaccine should be considered ineffective after 20 days of continuous exposure to higher temperatures ($t \geq 25^0C$), no matter the formulation used. However, this result needs to be verified through laboratory experiments. The results will be used to refine the model defined and introduced in this work (for the given vaccine), and will then be validated through actual observations on selected vaccine formulations.

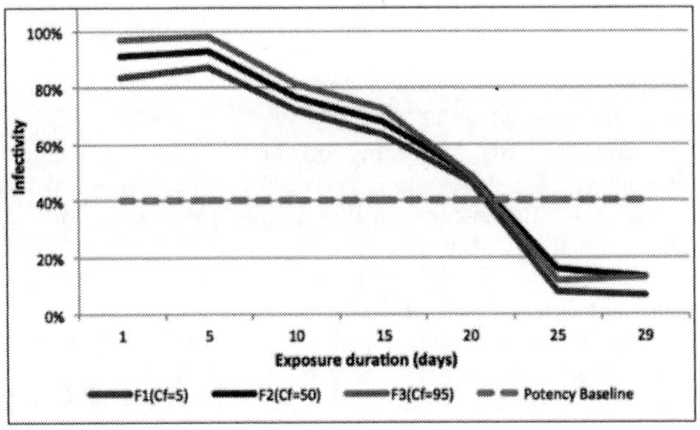

Figure 4. OPV infectivity simulation results at $t = 25^0C$ for 3 formulations

VI. Conclusion and Future Work

An innovative, semantically-enabled framework for knowledge and behavior specification, modeling and processing for vaccine systems engineering has been presented in this paper. This work is motivated by the limitations of current vaccine development approaches in capturing, representing and reconciling domains and disciplines knowledge and viewpoints across the vaccine development life cycle in an effective manner. As a result, vaccine development is a long, complex, and costly process that often results (when it succeeds) in vaccines whose potency is hard to predict and expensive to preserve. Current limitations are compounded by the highly stochastic nature of biological components involved (e.g., vaccines, pathogens) and knowledge disconnect between chemists, biologists, clinicians and the public stemming mostly from the lack of intuitive understanding of biological components and processes. In this work, we have shown that the implementation of a knowledge-driven framework is a promising and feasible solution that can result into successful vaccine systems engineering. Data and semantic models of domains supported by sound theories and tightly coupled with Markov Chain models of biological systems are the cornerstone of our approach. A key benefit is the ability to represent the system at various levels of abstractions in conformance to stakeholder viewpoints and the problem at hand. The core capabilities of the framework have been successfully demonstrated in a prototype vaccine preservation study.

Bringing the benefits of the framework introduced in this work to day-to-day work of stakeholders across the VDLC necessitates further work. This should include the refinement and validation of the framework for various vaccine types, analyses and cross-cutting concerns (e.g., potency, preservation, safety) and various environmental conditions. Design of experiments (as indicated in Topic 1) and actual laboratory, production and field assessment will be needed. Collaboration between stakeholders (including Systems Engineers) along the VDLC needs to be fostered in the development of domain and discipline knowledge used by the framework. An expansion of ongoing efforts in ontology development (e.g., vaccine ontology) is highly suitable [20].

References

[1] D. Endy, Foundations for Engineering Biology, Nature vol. 438, no. 24, pp. 449 - 453, 2005.

[2] The United Nation Children's Fund (UNICEF), Vaccines: Handled with Care, Division of Communication, New York, USA , 2004.

[3] Pharmaceutical Research and Manufacturing of America(PhRMA), Vaccines Factbook, PhRMA, 2013.

[4] World Health Organization(WHO), Six misconceptions about immunization, Accessible at : http://www.who.int/vaccine_safety/initiative/detection/immunization_misconceptions/en/ ; Retrieved: April 13, 2018.

[5] C. Rueckert and C. A. Guzman, "Vaccines: from empirical development to rational design", PLoS Pathog 8(11):e1003001. https://doi.org/10.1371/journal.ppat.1003001, 2012.

[6] F. Baader, I. Horrocks, and U. Sattler, Description Logics, In: Handbook of Knowledge Representation, pp. 135 - 180, Elsevier (US), 2008.

[7] I. Horrocks and Z. Pan, "RDFS(FA): Connecting RDF(S) and OWL DL", IEE Transactions on knowledge and data engineering, vol. 19, no. 02, pp. 192 - 206 (US), 2007.

[8] L. Petnga and M. A. Austin, '"An Ontological Framework for knowledge modeling and decision support in cyber-physical systems", Advanced Engineering Informatics, vol. 30, no. 1, pp. 77-94 (US), 2016.

[9] B. Ingalls, Mathematical Modeling in Systems Biology: An Introduction, Applied Mathematics, University of Waterloo, CA, 2012.

[10] C. J. Tomlin and J. D. Axelrod, "Biology by numbers: mathematical modeling in developmental biology", Nature Reviews; Genetics 8: pp. 331 - 340, 2007.

[11] M. Mosteller, M. A. Austin, R. Ghodssi, and S. Yang "Platforms for engineering experimental biomedical systems", 22th Annual INCOSE International Symposium (IS 2012), Rome, Italy, July 9-12, 2012.

[12] P. Delgoshaei, M.A. Austin, and A. Pertzborn, "A Semantic framework for modeling and simulation of cyber-physical systems", International Journal On Advances in Systems and Measurements, vol. 7, no. 3-4, pp. 223238 (EU), 2014.

[13] D. S. McVey, J. E. Galvin, and S. C. Olson, "A review of the effectiveness of vaccine potency control testing", International Journal for Parasitology, vol. 33, no. 5-6, pp. 507 - 516., 2003.

[14] H. Draayer, "Overview of currently approved veterinary vaccine potency testing methods and methods in development that do not require animal use", Procedia in Vaccinology, vol. 5 (2011) pp. 171 174 , 2011.

[15] U.S. Food and Drug Administration (FDA), Generally Recognized As Safe (GRAS) food substances, Accessible at : https://www.accessdata.fda.gov/scripts/fdcc/?set=SCOGS; Retrieved: April 13, 2018.

[16] A. Galaska, J. Milstien, and M. Zaffran, Thermostability of Vaccines, World Health Organization, Geneva, 1998.

[17] World Health Organization (WHO), Vaccination: Rattling the Supply Chain, Bulletin of the World Health Organization(WHO), vol. 89 (2011), pp. 324-325, 2011.

[18] I. Robinson, J. Webber, and E. Eifrem, Graph Databases: New opportunities for the connected data, O'Reilly Media, 224 pages, 2013.

[19] R. Wu, M.-M Georgescu, F. Delpeyroux, S. Guillot, J. Balanant, K. Simpson, and R. Crainic, "Thermostabilization of live virus vaccines by heavy water (D2O)", Vaccine, vol. 13, no. 12, pp. 1058 - 1063, 1995.

[20] University of Michigan School of Medicine, Vaccine Ontology, Accessible at : http://www.violinet.org/vaccineontology/introduction.php; Retrieved: April 13, 2018.

A Safe Graphics Rendering Solution for Consolidated Operating Systems

Angelos Mouzakitis*, Kevin Chappuis*, Julian Vetter*, Michele Paolino*, Youssef Kamoun* and Daniel Raho*
*Virtual Open Systems, Grenoble, France
Email: {a.mouzakitis,k.chappuis,j.vetter,m.paolino,y.kamoun,s.raho}@virtualopensystems.com

Abstract—**New breakthroughs in the automotive domain, such as Advanced Driver Assistance Systems (ADAS), 5G Vehicle to Everything (V2X) connections and In-Vehicle Infotainment (IVI) systems have made a significant impact on the automotive industry. Virtualization plays a key role in this trend, since it provides the ability to consolidate services with different levels of criticality, such as for instance ADAS functions and IVI or 5G connectivity services. Today, one scenario that arises with this new trend is the consolidation of a safety critical digital instrument cluster which displays safety metrics, e.g., speed, torque, etc. along with an IVI system. In such an architecture, the Graphical Processing Unit (GPU) is of central importance to ensure an efficient implementation. However, utilizing the GPU in both compartments raises safety concerns, and poses the question whether the strict isolation implemented by the virtualization layer can be upheld. Therefore, in this paper, we investigate this issue, and address it, by proposing a solution that consolidates a safety critical digital cluster along with an IVI system. We present the design of a safety mechanism to isolate the GPU rendering in both compartments, called "split-display", leveraging the ARM® TrustZone® technology. In our design, the secure world hosts a Real-Time Operating System (RTOS), which handles the GPU rendering in order to protect mission-critical tasks (e.g., speedometer and warning icons) from potential failures occurring in the IVI system. The mechanism provides safety guarantees for the GPU rendering of the RTOS. Our prototype "split-display" solution for mixed-criticality systems is implemented on the Renesas R-Car H3 platform. To validate our prototype implementation, we performed a number of experiments and evaluate the performance impact that occurs due to the consolidation. The results show that our implementation ensures at least 30 frames per second (fps) which is in line with the ISO 15005 safety standards. This number can even be achieved if a failure occurs in the IVI system.**

Keywords*–*Graphics; Split-Display; Mixed-Criticality; Real-Time; VOSYSmonitor

I. Introduction

Road vehicles nowadays are host to a huge number of embedded processors, executing millions of lines of code. However, the maintenance of these large code bases is tedious and error-prone for the vehicle manufacturers. Therefore, the manufacturers try to use off-the-shelf software wherever possible to facilitate and streamline their development process. The availability of existing Real Time Operating System (RTOS) solutions proves itself useful in this respect. Especially, since the OSEK/VDX [1]–[3] consortium certified some of these RTOSs as suitable for the use in vehicular embedded control units. Such OSEK/VDX-conforming RTOSs address the needs of the vehicle manufacturers in almost all concerns. They only fall short in a small but critical number of domains such as In-Vehicle Infotainment (IVI), security and safety. To address these shortcomings alternative RTOSs for the high-end automotive domain are available today.

But not only leveraging off-the-shelf software helps to streamline the development process of the vehicle manufacturers, also the integration of multiple components of different criticality (forming a so called Mixed Criticality System (MCS) [4]) lowers the number of embedded controllers in the car and consequently reduces cost, space, weight, heat generation and power consumption. By leveraging virtualization, the vehicle manufacturers can now run multiple systems on a single embedded controller, from a highly reliable RTOS for mission-critical functions to a highly customizable Linux-based system for IVI services.

Although, virtualization enables numerous new applications, the trend also poses new challenges on the software stack. One such challenge is the proper sharing of hardware resources. Since all software components access the same hardware components of the embedded controller, special care must be taken when integrating such an architecture. In the past, researchers have already shown how to undermine the isolation enforced by the OS using shared hardware resources (e.g., caches [5], DMA devices [6], etc). Thus, a resilient software architecture needs to be in place.

In this context we investigate the sharing of a common display among two components with different levels of criticality. This is not only challenging because the involved components (e.g., Video Signal Processor) are powerful embedded devices in itself, which have to be handled with care, to not jeopardise the system integrity. But the task is also urgent because a rich automotive user interface calls for the integration of an IVI along the instrument cluster.

In this paper we present a solution, integrated into an open source RTOS which composes multiple visual elements and renders them to a common display to meet the needs of future automotive applications in areas like IVI or security/safety. The system relies on the isolation properties enforced by a highly privileged software component called VOSYSmonitor [7], which guarantees isolation between peripherals and memory of both OSes using ARM® TrustZone®.

In particular, we make the following new contributions:

- We design a mixed criticality "split-display" solution to allow a mission critical instrument cluster to run side-by-side with an IVI system.
- we evaluate existing solutions, depict their advantages and drawbacks and position our novel approach among them.
- We implement a full prototype of our architecture and evaluate its performance on an automotive grade evaluation board (Renesas R-Car H3).

The rest of this paper is structured as follows. In Section II, we give background on virtualization, ARM® processor extensions and hypervisors in general. Then, in Section III we present related work and emphasize the advantages and drawbacks of existing solutions compared to our design. Our system architecture is described Section IV. Section V outlines our design. We focus on the peculiarities of our driver and automotive application in Section VI. We evaluate our design in Section VII. We conclude our work and present future work in Section VIII.

II. Background

In the following sections we give a brief overview of ARM® TrustZone®, ARM® Virtualization Extensions (VE) as well as the different types of hypervisors. We conclude this section with a concise introduction to VOSYSmonitor, which is the underlying firmware layer, providing the necessary isolation building blocks.

A. ARM TrustZone

Under the term TrustZone® [8], [9], ARM® introduced a new separation concept that is orthogonal to ELs (exception levels). This new concept provides two worlds, a "secure world" with the same set of ELs and a new mode, called monitor mode, to switch between this new and the classical "non-secure world" (Figure 1). The goal of TrustZone® is to keep the non-secure world fully backward compatible. Thus, the world separation and switching between worlds is almost fully implemented in hardware (with new sets of banked registers, etc). A new processor instruction was introduced with TrustZone®, the `smc` (Secure Monitor Call) instruction [10], to provide a way of interaction between both worlds. The isolation between the worlds is enforced in combination with other cooperating system components. A TrustZone® compliant memory controller announces the current security state ("secure" or "non-secure") for every bus transaction via the AXI AxPROT signal. Also, a new TrustZone® controller was introduced to allow for the configuration of certain ranges of physical memory as secure, preventing the non-secure world from accessing them. Moreover, the standard ARM® interrupt controller (GIC) supports the classification of interrupt sources into groups, allowing them to be routed to either the secure or non-secure world.

But it is important to note that the design of TrustZone® aims at a large degree of autonomy of both worlds, without the possibility (and perceived need) of close interaction. This means, as opposed to ARM VE, TrustZone® does not provide the ability to trap certain instructions, provide a nested paging mechanism or allow the direct injection of interrupts into specific virtual machines.

B. ARM Virtualization Extensions

ARM® added full virtualization support as an optional feature in ARMv7 [11]. Systems with these extensions have an additional execution mode, hypervisor mode (hyp). This mode is located in the new privilege level EL2, placed below EL0 and EL1. In addition, to having full access to all system control registers that exist in EL1, software executing in EL2 is provided with additional control registers for reconfiguring execution in EL0 and EL1, by, e.g., trapping certain instructions. ARM® VE also introduced a nested paging mechanism. This additional stage of translation, gives the hypervisor full control over the address space of systems executing in EL1.

It is worth noting that all EL2-controllable traps and the additional address translation only pertain to execution in the non-secure world, i.e., EL2 exists only in the non-secure world and its power does not extend beyond. However, the opposite holds: the monitor mode, in a processor incorporating TrustZone®, is able to access all non-secure EL2 controls.

C. Hypervisors

In general, hypervisors can be classified into two types: The Type-I hypervisor, also called bare-metal hypervisor, directly runs on the hardware without relying on a host operating system. Such a hypervisor has to bring its own set of device drivers and low-level system mechanisms (e.g., virtual memory management). Famous examples for such a hypervisor are Xen [13] or Hyper-V [14].

Type-II hypervisors on the other hand rely on a host operating system to run on. They leverage the operating system facilities which are already in place and run as a normal process. The host operating system however, has to corporate with the hypervisor process and, e.g., reflect specific types of exceptions back to this process. Famous examples for such a hypervisor are VirtualBox [15] or Parallels [16].

Kernel-based Virtual Machine (KVM) [17] is one of a few exception that do not allow a clear classification into one of the two types. In it's design it is a Type-I hypervisor, because it runs in a privileged mode (unlike a Type-II hypervisor), but as a Type-II hypervisor relies on a host operating system, in this case Linux.

D. VOSYSmonitor

VOSYSmonitor is a firmware that runs in the Secure Monitor mode (EL3) of ARMv8-A processors. It enables the native concurrent execution of two operating systems, such as, e.g., a safety critical RTOS along with a GPOS (General Purpose Operating System). The execution of both, 32-bit and 64-bit applications is possible and their isolation ensured by the means of TrustZone®.

Since VOSYSmonitor runs in EL3, the GPOS can still opt for a solution such as Linux-KVM, and leverage the ARM® VE to instantiate multiple VMs (Virtual Machines). Yet, the RTOS running in Secure world, is completely isolated from these applications executing in the normal world.

To ensure an efficient context switching between the two worlds hardware exception mechanisms, such as interrupts are used. Additionally, both OSs can voluntarily give up their execution time by invoking the `smc` instruction. VOSYSmonitor keeps tight control over these exceptions in order to ensure a proper operation of each world.

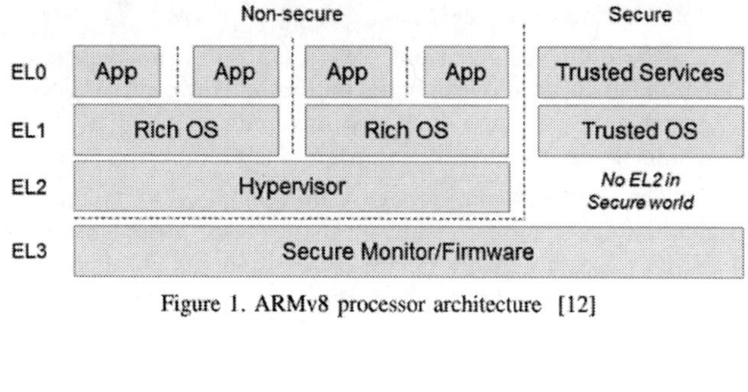

Figure 1. ARMv8 processor architecture [12]

III. Related Work

In the following section we present a number of projects or solutions which are relevant for this work.

In [18], Lee et al. describe an architecture called VADI which enables the execution of a digital instrument cluster on a consolidated hardware platform. The architecture is able to concurrently process graphic commands for two isolated execution domains using one Graphical Processing Unit (GPU) device that renders the frames on one display [19]. VADI implements a GPU sharing mechanism, while protecting the GPU and display device from non-trusted software applications by using TrustZone®.

Since physical virtualization is vulnerable to device driver failures, they leverage a virtualization solution called SASP, to consolidate the digital instrument cluster along with the IVI system. An RTOS, such as AUTOSAR [20] and a GPOS (e.g., Linux) can execute concurrently.

According to the evaluation phase, VADI maintains a performance of 30 frame per second (FPS) [21] [22], which is in line with the requirements for automotive control software. In addition, VADI ensures the execution of the digital instrument cluster component even in case of an unrecoverable failure of the other execution domain.

A framework that allows the sharing of a single GPU among different Virtual Machines (VMs), has been presented by Qi et al. [23]. The framework called VGRIS provides a GPU command queue for each VM in the main memory of the host OS. When an application calls a GPU API function the host OS intercepts the call and converts it into a specific command which is stored in the GPU command queue. The host OS runs a GPU scheduler which selects a specific queue and sends the commands to the GPU.

The evaluation of the Service Level Agreements (SLA) scheduling shows that the average FPS rates of the tested games, running in independent VMs are around 30 FPS. The drawback of VGRIS is, it depends on a Type 2 hypervisor because it is implemented in the host OS.

The VAGS architecture proposed by Gansel et al. [24] is an automotive display consolidation architecture which implements GPU virtualization in a vehicle. VAGS performs all graphic processing on a consolidated GPU device and draws the rendered frames on several display devices, such as the head unit screen, the center console, and the digital cluster.

VAGS consists of a Window Manager, which is based on a hierarchical access control management for display areas and input events. Therefore, the applications create, delete and move their windows through a dedicated Window Manager API. Depending on their permissions and priorities, applications are allowed to display their windows in dedicated display areas in order to avoid the overlapping of windows applications with different priorities.

The entire design from the virtualization manager to the graphical applications is based on Linux. However, VAGS only presents the design without any implementation and evaluation details since it is a work in progress solution.

The VMGL solution by Andres et al. [25] is the most popular GPU virtualization mechanism for virtual machines. VMGL uses a network device to send graphic commands to a virtualized GPU driver. The solution uses a standard network interface, such as a socket, and thus guarantees independence from the virtual platform. VMGL performance results closely resemble the results of their native counterparts.

The drawbacks of VMGL are, the following. Complex system configurations with multiple high-end applications, which concurrently render, may impose an aggregate bandwidth demand on VMGL of several Gbit/s. Moreover, the network communication requires a specific device and increases the transmission time of graphic commands between VMs since additional network processing and data copies are needed. In addition, automotive systems require device isolation to protect devices from errors caused by non-critical applications. Therefore, a system with VMGL must provide an additional isolation mechanism for the network device. Moreover, the VMGL mechanism is implemented on Xen [13] and VMware for the x86 architecture. But graphic libraries for embedded systems such as OpenGL ES and EGL are very different from libraries for x86 desktop systems like OpenGL and GLUT, thus further complicating the integration of VMGL into an automotive software stack.

IV. Architecture

The study of related work already highlights the requested functionality for rich graphical automotive applications, and also stresses the challenges that arise when consolidating such a system. Based on these requirements, we present our solution

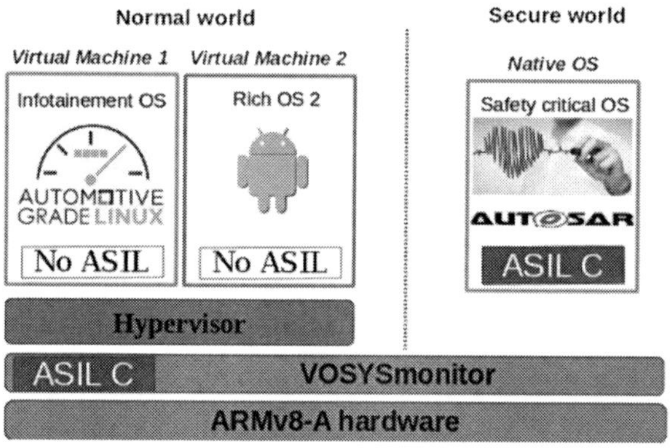

Figure 2. Automotive Architecture

in the following section.

Our architecture allows the rendering of content from both execution domains on a common physical screen. To achieve a high responsiveness of the digital instrument cluster we ported an open-source RTOS (i.e., FreeRTOS [26]) to run on top of VOSYSmonitor in the secure world while we rely on the high customizability of Linux in the normal world. Apart from ensuring a strict spatial and temporal isolation of the RTOS running in the Secure world, VOSYSmonitor also ensures a proper execution of the RTOS, when the non-critical application in the normal world fails.

The IVI system is composed of several components. It provides a rich interactive map that shows detailed route information, allows route planning, and also offers direction indicators for the driver. Along the map application which is integrated into a Linux system, we execute a virtualized Android VM to provide an off-the-shelf car infotainment system, paired with controls for interacting with the air conditioning system, a calling application or a video player. The digital instrument cluster on the other hand is implemented in the RTOS and is responsible for rendering mission critical information, such as the accelerometer, the tachometer and different warning icons for the temperature, missing seatbelts, etc. Figure 2 shows our architecture and the placement of the different components in the MCS. VOSYSmonitor constitutes the highest privileged component in the system, on top of which two operating systems are consolidated.

V. Design and Implementation

In Section IV, we described the high-level system architecture, and the placement of the components. Now we take a closer look, on how a safe interaction between the IVI and the instrument cluster is ensured by our architecture.

Figure 3 gives a detailed view on the vital system components. In Figure 3, it can be noticed that the GPU driver is

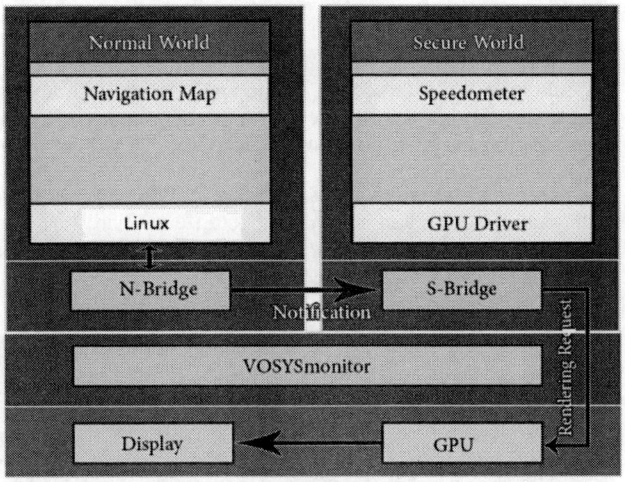

Figure 3. System Architecture

only available to the secure domain, thus requiring a routing mechanism to allow the normal world applications to interact with the graphic buffer as well. To achieve this, we designed two components, the S-Bridge for the secure and the N-Bridge for the normal world. These two components allow for an efficient message transfer between the normal and secure world. Notifications that are issued in the normal world, are routed to the secure world via the `smc` instruction. On top of which we use the concept of Remote Procedure Calls (RPC), to allow the normal world to invoke the desired functionality. That is, accessing GPU resources from the normal world, relies on invoking notifications from the N-Bridge to the S-Bridge. The Secure world then forwards the rendering requests to the GPU, which is in charge to render graphical content to the non-secure framebuffer.

While calls to the GPU are forwarded to the secure world, the planes are managed individually by the according OS (either RTOS or Linux). But, there are two dedicated display areas for the secure and normal world which are mapped to a depth level representing the priority of the plane. The concept is depicted in Figure 4. The figure shows the placement of the two framebuffers (planes) on the display. The plane with the higher priority is displayed on top of the one with the lower priority. So in our case, the RTOS is able to render on top of the Linux (which is displayed on the lower plane). Such a hierarchical management for display areas ensures that mission critical information are never cloaked by IVI content.

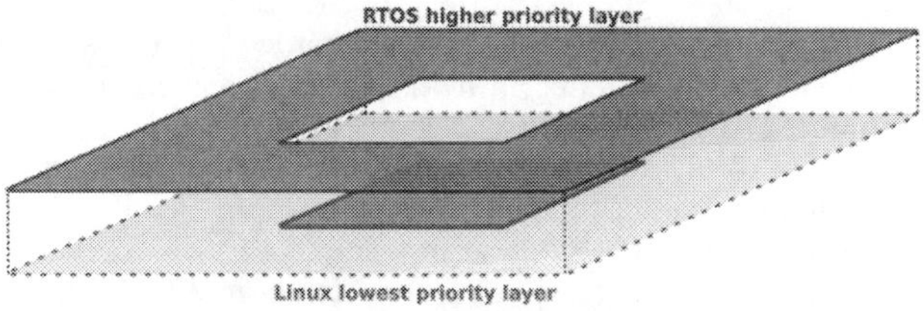

Figure 4. Display controller composition

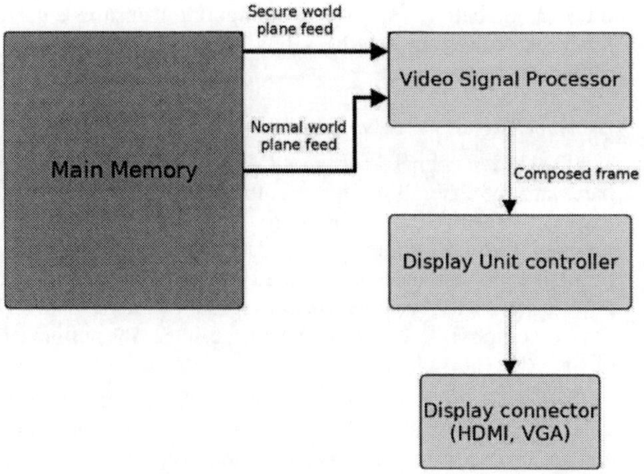

Figure 5. Hardware peripherals involved in the graphics pipeline

To summarize the design of our "split-display" architecture, the overall system implementation relies on the isolation capabilities of VOSYSmonitor (which makes sure that hardware peripherals needed for graphic rendering are only accessible from the secure world), a set of modified drivers that operate in the Secure world as well as the S-Bridge and N-Bridge. The design of the drivers allows both compartments to share the hardware peripherals that are involved in the graphics pipeline, while respecting the constraints imposed by the ISO 15005 standard for a safe display solution.

VI. Drivers & Automotive Application

In this section we discuss the different driver components as well as their implementation. But in order to understand the interaction of the driver components, we first have to take a look at the hardware peripherals that are involved in the graphics pipeline.

A. *Hardware peripherals*

Figure 5 illustrates the high level overview of the hardware peripherals that are used by the graphics rendering pipeline. The Renesas R-Car H3 contains multiple instances of these hardware components in order to forward rendered content to up to four different physical display connectors (VGA, LVDS and two HDMI) in parallel.

Our architecture ensures that all hardware peripherals and resources that are affected by the graphics rendering pipeline (direct or indirect), are isolated and protected from malicious activity of the normal world. VOSYSmonitor ensures this by configuring the memory address space of the peripherals that are driven by the RTOS using TrustZone®, to only allow "secure" accesses to the memory. Moreover, VOSYSmonitor also applies memory protection to peripherals related to the power domain configuration, clock generation, the system reset hardware block as well as the memory area used by the RTOS framebuffer. This system configuration ensures a correct rendering behaviour for the safety critical information at all times.

B. Video Signal Processor driver

The Video Signal Processor (VSP) peripheral is the core hardware peripheral to achieve the concept of the "split-display". The VSP is capable to read data from the main memory, through an intermediate data compression peripheral, through up to five independent read channels. Each read channel transfers data, which corresponds to a different plane. The device composes a frame based on the internal configuration of the composed planes.

The VSP driver operates in the RTOS and initializes the device with a static configuration for the operational clock and for properties of each read channel. Properties of the read channel include, e.g., the framebuffer's starting address, the resolution, the color depth, the plane's size and position in the display. For demonstration purposes, the scenario that we evaluate in Section VII consists of an RTOS plane, which has the following properties: width = 1920, height = 1080 and is placed at (0, 0) on the screen. Similarly, the Linux's plane has the following configuration: width = 640 height = 480 and it is placed at (640, 300). In this context, Linux is able to render at its own plane, that is initialized by the RTOS, and thus preventing further configuration changes. Moreover, the isolation of the planes for the RTOS and the Linux system as well as the frame composition ensures that the normal world cannot render at a part of the display that is owned by the secure domain.

C. Display unit driver

The Display Unit (DU) peripheral is the component in the graphics pipeline, which receives the output from a VSP module and produces the desired output (i.e., frame) regarding the internal configuration timings. It is important to note that the RTOS drives the peripheral with the same security policy as the VSP module. In this scenario, the physical connector for the split-display screen output is the Video Graphics Array (VGA) and the resolution is configured to 1920x1080x32bpp utilizing the planes of both OSs.

D. Automotive application

The automotive application is highly decomposed. Figure 6 shows the individual components and how the aggregated image is generated. For the secure world, we adapted a digital instrument cluster to run in the RTOS. The adaption also required us to first convert the images used by the instrument cluster (i.e., speedometer, tachometer and warning icons) from an ordinary image format into a binary format (according to the properties required by the framebuffer), referencable as

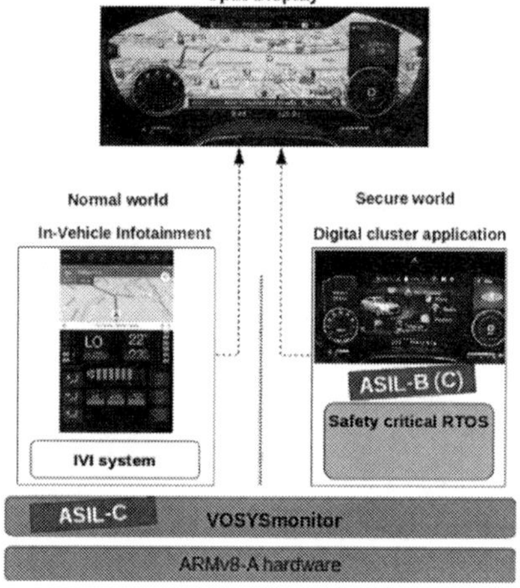

Figure 6. Automotive Application

symbols in the data section of the application. In the normal world we further decomposed the IVI components and added an additional layer of isolation by using the KVM hypervisors.

Our final setup is shown in Figure 7. Whereby, we routed the output of different components to different hardware ports. Table I gives an overview were each component IVI and instrument cluster was routed to.

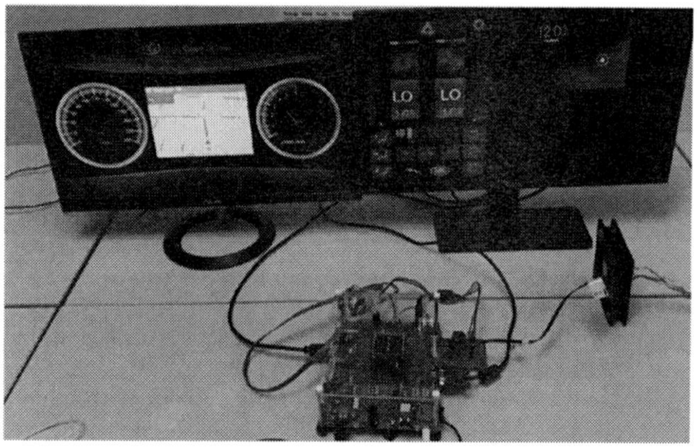

Figure 7. Evaluation board and display device

TABLE I. THE DIFFERENT APPLICATIONS OF THE IVI AND INSTRUMENT CLUSTER, WHERE THEY ARE PLACED IN THE SOFTWARE STACK AND THEIR OUTPUT DISPLAY.

Application	Component	Output Port
Secure application (Speedometer, Tachometer)	Instrument cluster (secure)	VGA
Navigation map	IVI (non-secure)	VGA
Control application for heating ventilation and air conditioning (HVAC)	IVI (non-secure)	HDMI 1
Android Lollipop (Hardware accelerated)	IVI (non-secure)	HDMI 2

VII. Evaluation

Our evaluation setup consisted of the following software components. In the normal world we executed a system based on Linux kernel version 4.4, while in the secure world we executed a FreeRTOS with a modified driver stack. We generated two realistic graphic workloads (as described in Section IV). The speedometer along with the tachometer in the secure world continuously rendered the vehicle's speed and engine torque. On the other hand we had the navigation map in the normal world showing detailed directions to the driver. These two applications represented our instrument cluster and IVI system, respectively. The entire graphical workload was being rendered using the CPU since FreeRTOS did not support GPU drivers for hardware acceleration.

Figure 7 depicts our hardware test setup. It consisted of a Renesas R-Car H3 [27] evaluation board. The board offers an automotive grade solution and features multiple ARM®-Cortex®-A57/A53 cores. The processing performance achieved by the hardware platform was 40,000 DMIPS (Dhrystone million instructions per second).

As shown in Figure 7, we split the display into two planes, one for the secure world and another one for the normal world. The upper plane displayed the speedometer, tachometer alongside the warning icons which were rendered by the Secure world, while the lower plane presented the navigation map of the normal world.

A. Rendering Time

This metric determines the number of frames that the CPU is able to render on the display. An important requirement in automotive industry is to ensure a minimum frame rate for critical information, such as the speed indicator and the warning icons. The purpose of this evaluation is to ascertain isolation between two graphical applications running in both worlds and that if a crash occurs in the normal world, performance of the Secure world is not impacted.

For the evaluation, the CPU rendering of the RTOS and the navigation map in the normal world are processed simultaneously, while a RTOS thread monitors the frames rendered per second by the RTOS.

Figure 8 indicates the performance of the Secure world running alongside the normal world and Figure 9 shows a result of the Secure world while the normal world remains idle. As shown in Figure 8, the frame rate of the digital cluster decreases whenever there is an animation and it is high when the animation stops. The animation requires frequent frame updates because it has to trace all new locations of the corresponding item (e.g., icons and the needle of the speedometer). Figure 9 shows that the secure world maintains a minimum frame rate of 30 fps even with a fault in the normal world. This means that the critical tasks running in the Secure world are completely isolated from the tasks running in the normal world. Moreover, in this evaluation, despite the fact that the navigation map is halted due to an unrecoverable fault (e.g., kernel fault) occurring in Linux, the speedometer remains running without any impact on its performance.

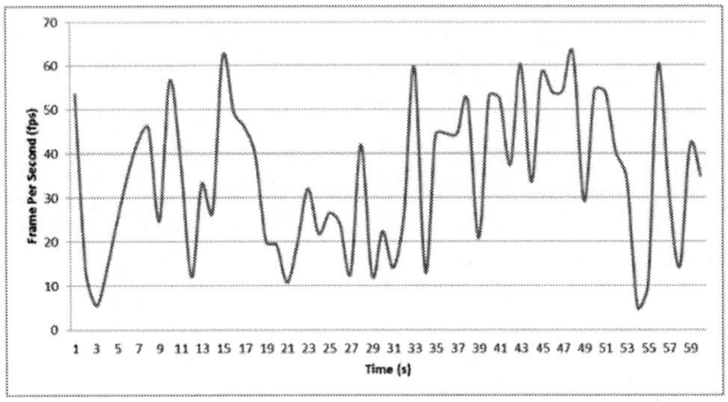

Figure 8. Performance of Digital cluster

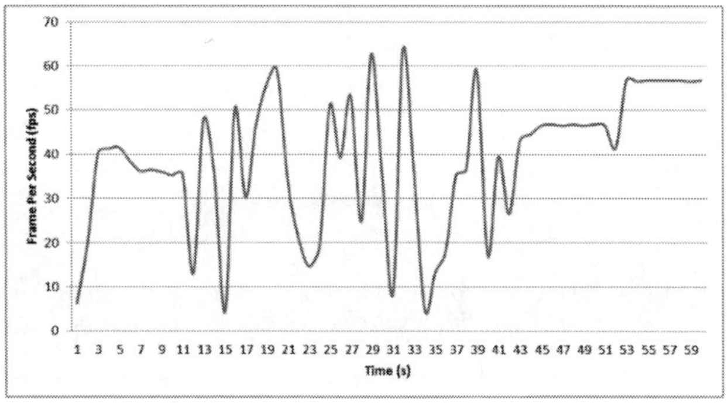

Figure 9. Performance of digital cluster when Linux fails

The above figures show that the Secure world maintains an average fps rate of 36.5, even when a fault occurs in the normal world, which is higher than the 30 fps minimum frame rate that is required to be able to have a smooth and fluid animation. The obtained results prove that there is a complete isolation between the two worlds without any world impacting the other's performance.

VIII. Conclusions and Future Work

In this paper we presented the "split display" architecture, a novel approach to tackle the issue of security and safety aware display sharing. Our architecture is based on VOSYSmonitor a highly privileged entity on top of which we integrated a Linux and an open source RTOS, functioning as our IVI and mission critical instrument cluster, respectively. Our architecture provides a strict isolation of the graphic applications running in the RTOS from the non-critical IVI running in the Linux. Although, our applications have been tested without graphical acceleration, our performance numbers still confirm our design decisions and clearly indicate the capability of our architecture to render mission critical information smoothly along with non-critical applications like a navigation map. We showed that even in the event of an unrecoverable failure in the normal world the mission critical instrument cluster is able to operate.

Our efforts included (but were not limited to) the design of two components called S-Bridge and N-Bridge to forward GPU rendering requests from the normal to the secure world, in the style of RPCs. Moreover, we ported several drivers critical for graphical rendering from Linux to FreeRTOS. We also developed and integrated a prototype of our architecture on an Renesas R-Car H3 evaluation board.

Since we implemented this prototype, there is no doubt about the feasibility of our approach.

In the future we want to focus our efforts on the following open points. First, sharing the graphic CPU rendering implementation with the FreeRTOS community. Second, improving the application to use a dedicated GPU and thus enabling graphical acceleration and increasing the overall FPS. Last, supporting the QT [28] graphical framework for the open source RTOS, to ease the creation of graphical applications.

IX. ACKNOWLEDGMENTS

This work has received funding from the European Union's Horizon 2020 research and innovation programme under the NGPaaS project (grant agreement No. 761557).

REFERENCES

[1] A. Zahir and P. Palmieri, "Osek/vdx-operating systems for automotive applications," in IEE Seminar on OSEK/VDX Open Systems in Automotive Networks (Ref. No. 1998/523), Nov 1998, pp. 4/1–418.

[2] D. John, "Osek/vdx history and structure," in IEE Seminar on OSEK/VDX Open Systems in Automotive Networks (Ref. No. 1998/523), Nov 1998, pp. 2/1–214.

[3] C. Hoffmann et al., "Osek/vdx network management," OSEK/VDX Open Systems in Automotive Networks (Ref. No. 1998/523), IEE Seminar, November 1998.

[4] A. Burns and R. Davis, "Mixed criticality systems - a review," Department of Computer Science, University of York, Tech. Rep, 2013, pp. 1–69.

[5] C. Percival, "Cache missing for fun and profit," BSDCan, 2005.

[6] R. Wojtczuk, J. Rutkowska, and A. Tereshkin, "Xen 0wning trilogy," Invisible Things Lab, 2008.

[7] P. Lucas, K. Chappuis, M. Paolino, N. Dagieu, and D. Raho, "Vosysmonitor, a low latency monitor layer for mixed-criticality systems on armv8-a," Euromicro Technical Committee on Real-Time Systems 2017, June 2017.

[8] T. Alves and D. Felton, "Trustzone: Integrated hardware and software security-enabling trusted computing in embedded systems (july 2004)."

[9] "ARM Security Technology - Building a Secure System using TrustZone Technology," Whitepaper, ARM Limited, April 2009.

[10] "Smc calling convention system software on arm platforms," Whitepaper, ARM Limited, November 2016.

[11] R. Mijat and A. Nightingale, "Virtualization is coming to a platform near you," ARM Limited.

[12] Armv8 processor architecture. [Online]. Available: https://community.arm.com [retrieved: April, 2018]

[13] P. Barham et al., "Xen and the art of virtualization," vol. 37, no. 5, 2003, pp. 164–177.

[14] Y. Haga, K. Imaeda, and M. Jibu, "Windows server 2008 r2 hyper-v server virtualization," Fujitsu Sci. Tech. J, vol. 47, no. 3, 2011, pp. 349–355.

[15] "Virtualbox," http://www.virtualbox.com, Oracle, March 2018.

[16] Parallels, "Parallels workstation, parallels desktop," http://www.parallels.com, March 2018.

[17] Qumranet, "Kernel-based virtual machine for linux," http://qumranet.com/kvm, March 2018.

[18] C. Lee, S. W. Kim, and C. Yoo, "Vadi: Gpu virtualization for an automotive platform," IEEE Transactions on Industrial Informatics, vol. 12, no. 1, 2016, pp. 277–290.

[19] C. Patsakis, K. Dellios, and M. Bouroche, "Towards a distributed secure in-vehicle communication architecture for modern vehicles," Computers & Security, vol. 40, 2014, pp. 60–74.

[20] S. Martínez-Fernández, C. P. Ayala, X. Franch, and E. Y. Nakagawa, "A survey on the benefits and drawbacks of autosar," in Proceedings of the First International Workshop on Automotive Software Architecture. ACM, 2015, pp. 19–26.

[21] F. Chao, S. He, J. Chong, R. B. Mrad, and L. Feng, "Development of a micromirror based laser vector scanning automotive hud," in Mechatronics and Automation (ICMA), 2011 International Conference on. IEEE, 2011, pp. 75–79.

[22] V. Milanovic, A. Kasturi, and V. Hachtel, "High brightness mems mirror based head-up display (hud) modules with wireless data streaming capability," vol. 9375, 2015, p. 93750A.

[23] Z. Qi et al., "Vgris: Virtualized gpu resource isolation and scheduling in cloud gaming," ACM Transactions on Architecture and Code Optimization (TACO), vol. 11, no. 2, 2014, p. 17.

[24] S. Gansel, S. Schnitzer, F. Dürr, K. Rothermel, and C. Maihöfer, "Towards virtualization concepts for novel automotive hmi systems," 2013, pp. 193–204.

[25] H. A. Lagar-Cavilla, N. Tolia, M. Satyanarayanan, and E. De Lara, "Vmm-independent graphics acceleration," 2007, pp. 33–43.

[26] FreeRTOS. Open source real time operating system. [Online]. Available: http://www.freertos.org [retrieved: January, 2003]

[27] Renesas. Rcar-h3. [Online]. Available: https://www.renesas.com/en-us/solutions/automotive/products/rcar-h3.html [retrieved: January, 2015]

[28] Qt. Cross-platform application framework. [Online]. Available: https://www.qt.io/ [retrieved: January, 1995]

System Performance Condition Curve Estimation Based on Data Analysis of the Taipei Metro System

Tzu-Chia Kao and Snow H. Tseng*
Department of Electrical Engineering,
National Taiwan University,
Taipei 10617, Taiwan
e-mails: b03901004@ntu.edu.tw, stseng@ntu.edu.tw

Abstract—**The Taipei Metro is still very young compared to the other metropolitan metro systems in the world. The data provided by Taipei Rapid Transit Corporation (TRTC) is analyzed, including: air conditioner, communication system, switcher, platform door, 22kV switchboard, Automated fare collection (AFC) door, Wenhu Line traffic control computer, Transmission system, elevator and escalator. The research objective is to assess the performance based on the one-year-long data from TRTC, to determine the equipment stage of its lifetime, and estimate the asset's remaining life and maintenance condition. Reported analysis of the data shows minute indication of the system current status; further analysis is in progress.**

Keywords-degradation; maintenance; metro; MRT; performance analysis.

I. Introduction

We analyze the maintenance record of the Taipei Mass Rapid Transit (MRT) system, which is a well maintained system renown worldwide for its tidiness, stability and efficiency. If the maintenance data can be analyzed to yield information about how to perfect the performance of the Taipei MRT system, the analysis can provide useful information to improving Taipei MRT, or, more generally, to assess the performance of other systems.

Since the MRT system of Taipei Rapid Transit Corporation (TRTC) is relatively young (began operation on March 28, 1996, a total of 22 years to date [1]), most of the equipment has not yet been replaced; the records of repair and maintenance are detailed and are stored in digital form. Thus, our research goal is to establish a degradation curve based on the maintenance and performance record, and use to assess the Taipei MRT system, and equipment of other metro systems. The performance and degradation of metropolitan metro systems have been the focus of general public. Various studies have been reported, including technical issues of the MRT. Rail track condition monitoring is an important technical concern of the MRT system [2]. However, it is infeasible to constantly inspect track conditions; an inspection once a month or less is more or less the usual maintenance. Severe track condition degradation that isn't detected early is a potential threat to the railway system. Hence, more attention has been devoted to monitoring track condition via in-service vehicles [3-5]. The general goal of the research and technical modifications is to improve the performance and reliability of a mass rapid transit system.

We also looked into some older subway systems on the Internet. As reported in [6], train R36 serviced from 1964 to 2003, a total of 39 years. R160s were used to replace 45-year-old trains. In another news report about the old trains [7], the oldest trains for New York City Subway were planned to serve for 58 years, and now this type of trains are actually found too old with very high failure rate and not appealing to meet passengers. From the limited reference that we can access, an estimate of the subway train lifetime is estimated to be around 40 to 50 years. For example, some lines of Singapore Mass Rapid Transit (SMRT) have been operating since 1987, 30 years from today. On the other hand, TRTC operated from 1996, which is only 21 years ago. There is a difference of 9 years. The assets' actual wear-out period may lie somewhere between 20 years (the oldest TRTC asset), and 40 years (New York City Subway). All these metropolitan metro systems are different in various aspects, thus, the characteristics of these MRT systems are expected to differ; the predictability and accuracy of the estimation and extrapolation based on TRTC to assess other MRT systems using the TRTC system data is understandably incomplete; with unknown number of variables involved, the accuracy of assessment may be very limited.

Assessment and quantification of the system current status is essential to enhance performance. The degradation curve is commonly employed for estimation of the system current status. Analysis of the reliability is commonly based on failure rate and maintenance records [8]. Based on the status of the system, possible improvement of the maintenance and performance can be assessed. By means of the degradation analysis the research objective is to shed light on enhancing the metro system performance.

To study the maintenance and performance characteristics, various approaches have been reported [9-18], including the popular bathtub curve analysis [19]-[24]. The Bathtub curve is commonly employed for system performance analysis [25]. Analysis based upon the bathtub curve has been extensively applied to various problems; various modifications to improve applicability have been reported [11][26]-[29]. It is suggested that bathtub curve could be interfered by human factor [30]; for example, if the asset retired in its early stage, the curve may not rise up during the wear-out period and may even descend. If properly maintained, the curve may not rise in the wear-out period, similar to the situation in airline industry. However, few MRT systems in reality exhibit degradation behavior similar to the bathtub curve model [31].

The rest of this paper is organized as follows. Section II describes the goal of this research project. Section III describes the research method. Section IV summarizes the data analysis; finally, a summary is presented in Section V, followed by an acknowledgement.

II. Research Goal

We proposed to thoroughly analyze the Taipei MRT data. We have data from Taipei MRT consisting of 11 systems: electric multiple unit (EMU), EMU air conditioner, EMU communication, switcher, platform door, 22kV switchboard, Automated fare collection (AFC) door, Wenhu Line traffic control computer, Transmission system, elevator, and escalator. By analyzing the dataset with various state-of-the-art approaches, such as deep learning, the research objective is to analyze the equipment present status and identify possible tendencies or features that may be indicative of the system performance.

III. Method

Ideally, analysis of the maintenance data would yield a simple bathtub-shaped degradation curve for each equipment. However, the bathtub-shaped degradation curve is a theoretical model; degradation curve of most cases do not follow the same degradation curve, not to mention each equipment may exhibit different characteristics. Furthermore, each equipment in the Taipei metro system consists of various brands and various models that may possess different intrinsic characteristics. Furthermore, since each equipment is maintained by human, the degradation curve is unlikely to be a simple universal bathtub-shaped curve. Thus, it is infeasible to come up with a universal bathtub-shaped degradation curve for each Taipei MRT equipment. Based on the experience we had from the initial attempt to analyze the data, we propose the following steps:

First, based upon the original maintenance records, calculate the duration between: 1) when the equipment was first engaged in operation, and, 2) the failure date. This time interval represents the duration of malfunction-free operation, which is also the time for a malfunction to take place. By analyzing the malfunction-free duration instead of the number of malfunctions each month may yield more realistic relationship.

Second, calculate the failure times per month to acquire the failure rate for each individual equipment. (For the equipment related to EMU, the failure rate is acquired by the failure time divided by the train mileage.)

Third, average each equipment's failure times to get the average failure rate. Use a statistical software to calculate the regression curve, and extrapolate for comparison with other metro system performance data.

Continue these steps to process another set of data accordingly; then compare the regression behavior. Analyze the difference between the two datasets.

IV. Data Analysis

Initial attempt of analysis is performed. We use the failure statistics for monthly failure rate provided by TRTC. The AFC gates statistics is shown in Figure 1; the averaged malfunction rate is calculated and shown in Figure 2. As shown in Figure 1, the equipment consists of mixed brand, model, age; thus, the total number of malfunctions is not representative of individual equipment.

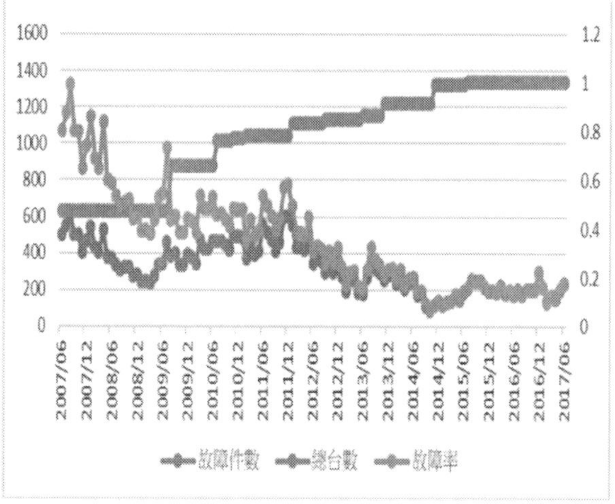

Figure 1. Failure rate of AFC gates vs. time. The failure rate decreases monotonically with time.

Based upon the trend of the data, the failure rate has been declining yearly until it reaches low and stable end tail. Possible factors are speculated, this mostly likely is due to the improvement of MRT maintenance. On the other hand, since the age of each equipment and the number of samples for each equipment are not consistent, the total failure rate is not a fair representation of a specific individual equipment. Thus, we target to analyze the age's effect of the individual equipment as far as possible.

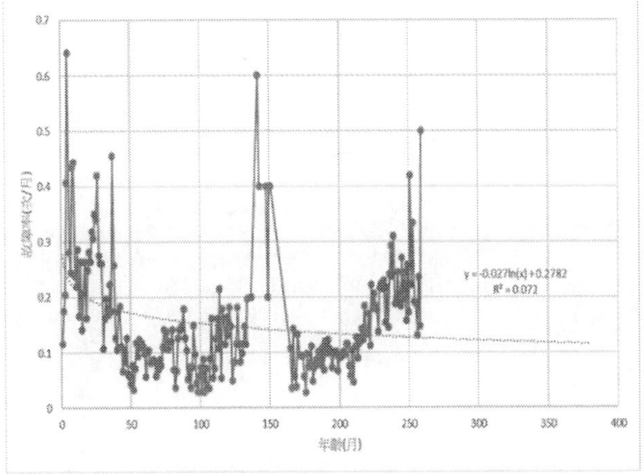

Figure 2. The averaged malfunction rate of the AFC gate *vs*. time.

With sufficient data for escalators and elevators, we try to quantify the failure rate vs. the age for each individual equipment with correlation analysis. On the other hand, for some equipment that seem to have no variation among one another, e.g., EMU, platform door, switcher and 22kV switchboard, we propose to calculate the failure rate vs. failure date. As shown in Figure 2., for the Wenhu line Central control computers, AFC gates and Transmission system, due to lack of sufficient data, the failure rate vs. failure date is analyzed. The malfunction rate decreases then later increases, exhibiting behavior similar to a bathtub curve. The spikes at the center is likely due to lack of sufficient data points to reveal detail trend.

V. CONCLUSION

The data provided by TRTC contains no more than malfunctions each month; furthermore, there is no severity information of the malfunction event. For a complex system, such as MRT, which involves enormous number of factors including human, there are all kinds of characteristics exhibited by the system in complex ways. Thus, it is infeasible to determine the system status with just a single variable. Nevertheless, undoubtedly a rich amount of information is contained in the maintenance data. We believe the data contains rich information and can be further harnessed, possibly with big data analysis, to yield more information that may be essential to enhance the MRT performance.

ACKNOWLEDGMENT

We thank TRTC for providing information data for analysis and support to make this project possible. This research is supported by the Taiwan National Science Council Grant 106-2112-M-002-008 and National Taiwan University grant NTU-ERP-103R89086.

REFERENCES

[1] "Taipei Metro," *Wikipedia*.

[2] X. K. Wei, F. Liu, and L. M. Jia, "Urban rail track condition monitoring based on in-service vehicle acceleration measurements," *Measurement*, vol. 80, pp. 217-228, Feb 2016.

[3] M. Molodova, M. Oregui, A. Nunez, Z. L. Li, and R. Dollevoet, "Health condition monitoring of insulated joints based on axle box acceleration measurements," *Engineering Structures*, vol. 123, pp. 225-235, Sep 2016.

[4] G. Lederman, S. H. Chen, J. Garrett, J. Kovacevic, H. Y. Noh, and J. Bielak, "Track-monitoring from the dynamic response of an operational train," *Mechanical Systems and Signal Processing*, vol. 87, pp. 1-16, Mar 2017.

[5] R. Jiang *et al.*, "Network operation reliability in a Manhattan-like urban system with adaptive traffic lights," *Transportation Research Part C-Emerging Technologies*, vol. 69, pp. 527-547, Aug 2016.

[6] Metropolitan Transportation Authority. (2017). *New York City Transit - History and Chronology*. Available: http://web.mta.info/nyct/facts/ffhist.htm

[7] D. Rivoli. (2015). *Ancient subway trains on C and J/Z lines won't be replaced until 2022, documents say*. Available: http://www.nydailynews.com/new-york/ancient-subway-trains-won-replaced-2022-article-1.2323289

[8] H. Yin, K. Wang, Y. Qin, Q. Hua, and Q. Jiang, "Reliability analysis of subway vehicles based on the data of operational failures," *EURASIP Journal on Wireless Communications and Networking*, journal article vol. 2017, no. 1, p. 212, December 15 2017.

[9] Z. G. Li, J. G. Zhou, and B. Y. Liu, "System Reliability Analysis Method Based on Fuzzy Probability," *International Journal of Fuzzy Systems*, vol. 19, no. 6, pp. 1759-1767, Dec 2017.

[10] A. Z. Afify, G. M. Cordeiro, N. S. Butt, E. M. M. Ortega, and A. K. Suzuki, "A new lifetime model with variable shapes for the hazard rate," *Brazilian Journal of Probability and Statistics*, vol. 31, no. 3, pp. 516-541, Aug 2017.

[11] T. Kamel, A. Limam, and C. Silvani, "Modeling the degradation of old subway galleries using a continuum approach," *Tunnelling and Underground Space Technology*, vol. 48, pp. 77-93, Apr 2015.

[12] D. Brancherie and A. Ibrahimbegovic, "Novel anisotropic continuum-discrete damage model capable of representing localized failure of massive structures: Part I: theoretical formulation and numerical implementation," *Engineering Computations*, vol. 26, no. 1-2, pp. 100-127, 2009.

[13] R. Tahmasbi and S. Rezaei, "A two-parameter lifetime distribution with decreasing failure rate," *Computational Statistics & Data Analysis*, vol. 52, no. 8, pp. 3889-3901, Apr 2008.

[14] C. F. Daganzo and N. Geroliminis, "An analytical approximation for the macroscopic fundamental diagram of urban traffic," *Transportation Research Part B-Methodological*, vol. 42, no. 9, pp. 771-781, Nov 2008.

[15] C. Kus, "A new lifetime distribution," *Computational Statistics & Data Analysis*, vol. 51, no. 9, pp. 4497-4509, May 15 2007.

[16] C. D. Lai, M. Xie, and D. N. P. Murthy, "A modified Weibull distribution," *IEEE Transactions on Reliability*, vol. 52, no. 1, pp. 33-37, Mar 2003.

[17] O. O. Aalen and H. K. Gjessing, "Understanding the shape of the hazard rate: A process point of view," *Statistical Science*, vol. 16, no. 1, pp. 1-14, Feb 2001.

[18] S. Kotz and D. N. Shanbhag, "Some new approaches to probability distributions," *Advances in Applied Probability*, vol. 12, no. 4, pp. 903-921, 1980 1980.

[19] S. K. Maurya, A. Kaushik, S. K. Singh, and U. Singh, "A new class of distribution having decreasing, increasing, and bathtub-shaped failure rate," *Communications in Statistics-Theory and Methods*, vol. 46, no. 20, pp. 10359-10372, 2017.

[20] Q. H. Duan and J. R. Liu, "Modelling a Bathtub-Shaped Failure Rate by a Coxian Distribution," *IEEE Transactions on Reliability*, vol. 65, no. 2, pp. 878-885, Jun 2016.
[21] W. J. Roesch, "Using a new bathtub curve to correlate quality and reliability," *Microelectronics Reliability*, vol. 52, no. 12, pp. 2864-2869, Dec 2012.
[22] J. Navarro and P. J. Hernandez, "How to obtain bathtub-shaped failure rate models from normal mixtures," *Probability in the Engineering and Informational Sciences*, vol. 18, no. 4, pp. 511-531, 2004 2004.
[23] S. Rajarshi and M. B. Rajarshi, "Bathtub distributions - a review," *Communications in Statistics-Theory and Methods*, vol. 17, no. 8, pp. 2597-2621, 1988 1988.
[24] M. V. Aarset, "How to identify an bathtub hazard rate," *IEEE Transactions on Reliability*, vol. 36, no. 1, pp. 106-108, Apr 1987.
[25] K. L. Wong, "The bathtub does not hold water any more," *Quality and Reliability Engineering International*, vol. 4, no. 3, pp. 279-282, 1988.
[26] H. T. Zeng, T. Lan, and Q. M. Chen, "Five and four-parameter lifetime distributions for bathtub-shaped failure rate using Perks mortality equation," *Reliability Engineering & System Safety*, vol. 152, pp. 307-315, Aug 2016.
[27] F. K. Wang, "A new model with bathtub-shaped failure rate using an additive Burr XII distribution," *Reliability Engineering & System Safety*, vol. 70, no. 3, pp. 305-312, Dec 2000.
[28] D. N. P. Murthy and R. Jiang, "Parametric study of sectional models involving two Weibull distributions," *Reliability Engineering & System Safety*, vol. 56, no. 2, pp. 151-159, May 1997.
[29] G. S. Mudholkar, D. K. Srivastava, and M. Freimer, "The exponentiated Weibull family - A reanalysis of the bus-motor-failure data," *Technometrics*, vol. 37, no. 4, pp. 436-445, Nov 1995.
[30] T. Cheng, "A Critical Discussion on Bath-tub Curve," presented at the 42nd Chinese society for quality annual meeting and 12th National Quality Management Seminar, 2006.
[31] G. A. Klutke, P. C. Kiessler, and M. A. Wortman, "A critical look at the bathtub curve," *IEEE Transactions on Reliability*, vol. 52, no. 1, pp. 125-129, 2003.

Implementation of a Scenario-based Energy Saving Mechanism in Smart Lighting Systems

Jung-Sik Sung, Dae Ho Kim, and Seonghee Park
IoT Research Department, ETRI
Daejeon, Korea
email: jssung@etri.re.kr, dhkim7256@etri.re.kr, pshee@etri.re.kr

***Abstract*—A smart lighting system solution that optimizes the energy is required for energy saving. It should control lighting based on time and space, and it should be context-aware. In this study, we propose a scenario-based energy-saving mechanism based on the user's behavior patterns and situations in order to reduce significantly the energy consumption compared to the conventional Light Emitting Diode (LED) lighting in buildings. In addition, we built 10 test bed unit spaces for our test bed that were controlled automatically. Through evaluation, the scenario-based smart lighting system test bed presented in this study proved to be about 54% better than conventional LED lighting in terms of energy saving.**

Keywords- smart lighting system; energy saving; internet of things; LED.

I. Introduction

The proportion of energy consumption by lighting in Korea reaches 20% [1]. In particular, the amount of energy consumed in buildings accounts for more than 30% of total energy consumption. As the national government prohibits the use of incandescent lamps, replacement of incandescent lamps and fluorescent lamps with LED lighting is increasing [2]. By replacing the existing fluorescent lamp with LED lighting, it is possible to reduce the energy by 30%, and when using dimmable LED lighting, energy savings of about 50% are possible [1]. However, in order to save energy, a smart lighting solution can be developed and popularized to optimize energy consumption through lighting control based on time, situation, and space to enhance user satisfaction by supporting customized service, and suitable for the situation instead of simply replacing with LED lighting [3]. In this study, we propose a scenario-based energy saving mechanism suitable for user 's behavior pattern and situation in order to reduce energy consumption much more than conventional LED lighting in the unit space of a building.

The remainder of this paper is organized as follows. Section II describes the smart lighting system architecture. In Section III, scenarios appropriate to the behavioral patterns of each unit space are described. In Section IV shows energy saving performance measured in each unit space. Finally, conclusions are discussed in Section V.

II. Design of Smart Lighting System Architecture

The purpose of this study is to utilize a smart lighting system to provide users with functional, human conformity, emotional satisfaction and realize energy savings. For this purpose, ten unit spaces, such as an office, a conference room, a restroom, a hallway, parking lots, a staff lounge, stairwells, a lobby, a cafe, and a development room (lab) are selected, and user behavior patterns are defined for each unit space. We constructed a test bed to control the lighting according to each unit space and environment. The test bed in the unit space is designed to allow the user to directly control the lighting using the smart pad. It can also be controlled automatically without user intervention for 24 hours based on scenarios such as environmental events, schedule, and user behavior patterns.

Figure 1 shows a network configuration of a smart lighting system. The management server can control the lighting through the gateway, and the sensors transmit the event to the management server through the gateway when the event occurs. In addition, power consumption is measured by Current Transformer (CT) sensor in each unit space, and it is transmitted to the management server or service servers through the metering gateway so that the amount of power consumed in real time in each unit space can be monitored.

III. Scenario Design Appropriate to Behavior Patterns in Unit Space

In this study, the scenarios of 10 unit spaces for user convenience and energy saving were defined for behaviors and events. The behavior of each space was derived through the survey of major act patterns by space and empirical test subjects [4]-[6]. Table 1 shows the behavioral scenarios for the three unit spaces, such as office, restroom, and stairwells among 10 unit spaces. In Table 1, the main activities in the office were defined as weekly work, lunch, and night work, and the scenarios were designed so that the lighting of the office could be appropriately controlled according to the main activity. The main behaviors in the restroom were defined as the activities, such as entrance, toilet, washing and color temperature control according to the season. In the stairwells, scenarios for the entrance, movement, and fire occurrences were designed.

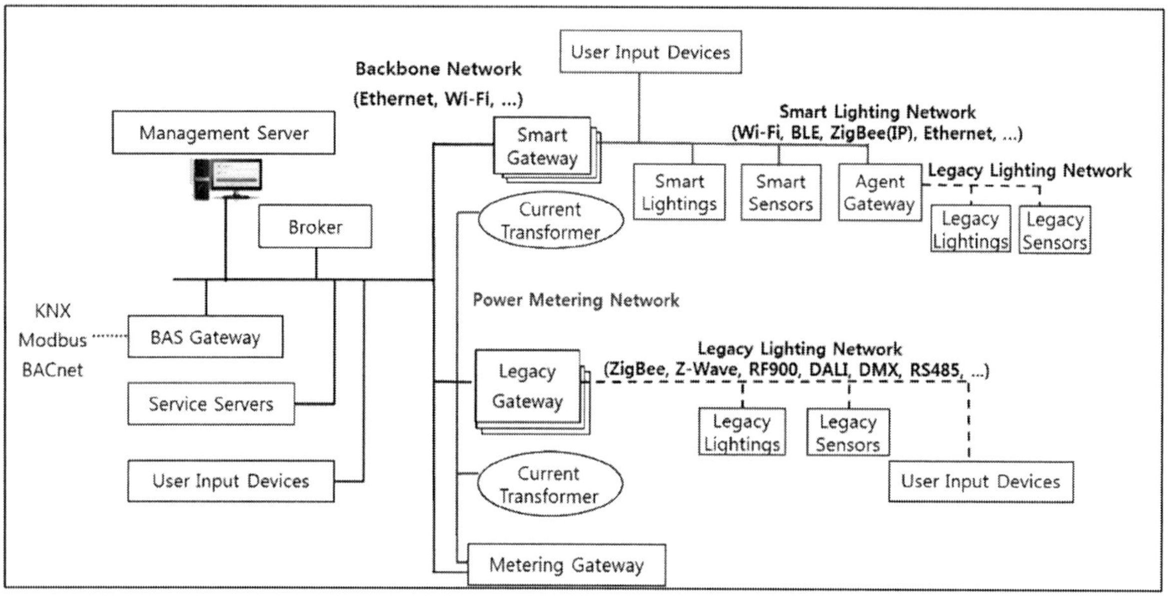

Figure 1. Configuration of smart lighting system

TABLE I. DESIGN OF SCENARIOS IN ACCORDING TO ACTIVITIES

Space	Behavior/ Event	Scenario
Office	Day work	Turn on all lights if there are occupants. Automatically adjusts the brightness of lights according to the amount of daylight. Turn off all lights if there is no occupant.
	Lunch	If there are occupants, dimming to 20-25% of working time brightness.
	Night work	Illuminates above occupant seat by human body detection. (3 ~ 5m from user's spot keeps 20 ~ 25% illumination, Turn off if it is more than 5m away from the user' s spot) Turn off the corresponding lights if there is no occupant.
Restroom	Entrance	Lights are illuminated by each zone through human body detection. Lights are turned off for each zone when no human body is detected.
	Toile	Lighting in individual partition by human body detection when entering individual partition.
	Wash/Mirror	The ceiling lights and indirect lights are turned on when washing hands or approaching the vanity unit to see the mirror.
	Four seasons	Spring/Autumn 4000K, Summer 5000K, Winter 3000K
Stairwells	Entrance	When a person opens the door of a stairway, the light upstairs and downstairs including that floor are turned on. (The brightness of the lighting on the floor where the person is located is 150 lux, Upper/lower floors apply 50%)
	Movement	Identify the person's position and direction of movement so that the floor in the direction in which the person is moving gradually becomes bright. In this case, the lighting brightness is the same as the entrance
	Fire occurrence	If a fire is detected by a sensor, a fire alarm is sent to the management server through the gateway. Detects the human body and informs the management server through the gateway of the position of the evacuator. The escapable floors connected to the outside are brightly lit at 150 lux and the other floors lit at 30 lux. Illuminates the current number of floors on the wall and illuminates the arrow lights to induce evacuation.

IV. ENERGY SAVING EVALUATION

In order to investigate the real -time power consumption in each unit space, we measured the power consumption by attaching CT sensors to the switchboard of the test bed.

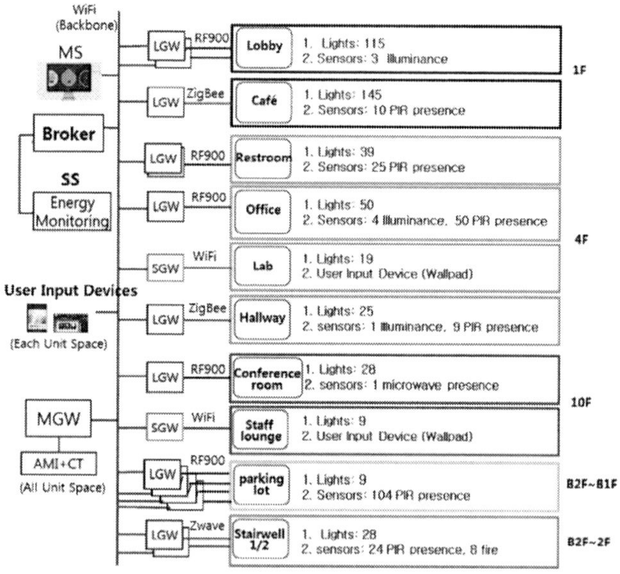

Figure 2. Test bed configuration for evaluation.

We implemented the system so that the physical quantities (target illuminance, use time, dimming) of each behavior can be matched as much as possible. Also, we evaluated the energy saving rate compared to LED lighting by measuring the energy amount satisfying the illuminance value for each unit space. Figure 2 shows the test bed configuration for energy saving evaluation.

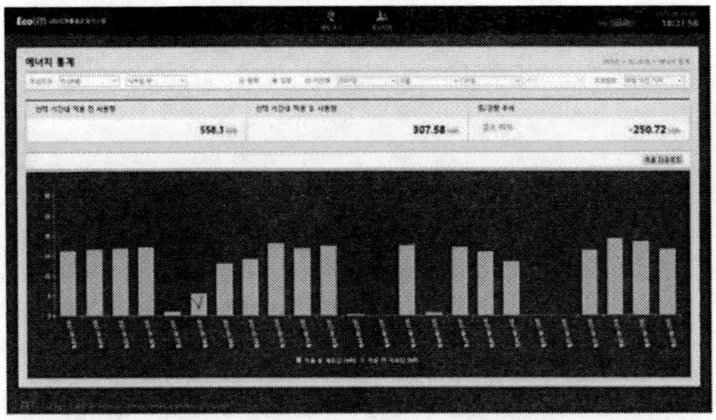

Figure 3. Real-time energy consumption monitoring in the office room.

Figure 3 shows how the management server monitors the energy consumption measured in the office every one minute. The dotted line represents the power consumption for the conventional LED lighting, and the bar represents the power consumption when controlling the LED lighting based on behavioral scenarios using the smart lighting system. Compared with real-time power consumption data of about 25 minutes, it shows 45% energy saving rate compared to LED lighting.

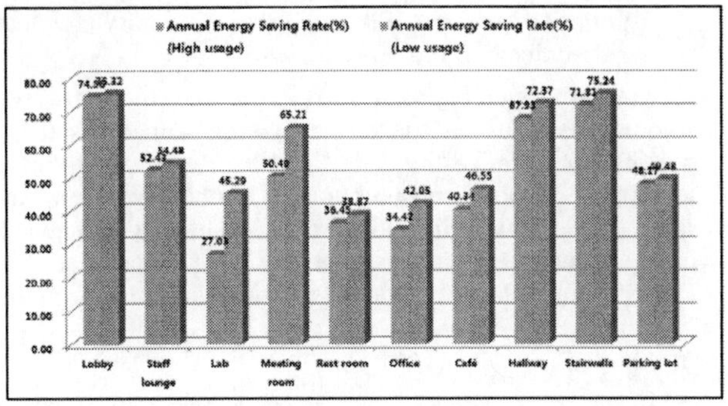

Figure 4. Anuual energy saving rate of proposed mechanism.

Figure 4 shows the annual energy saving rate for each unit space when applying the scenario-based mechanism presented in this study against existing LED lighting. For each unit space, the bar graph on the left shows annual energy saving rate when the behavior frequency is high, and the right bar graph shows annual energy saving rate when the behavior frequency is low.

V. CONCLUSION

In this study, a smart lighting system test bed is constructed for 10 unit spaces of a building to provide users with functional, human conformity, emotional satisfaction and realize energy savings. We defined behavior patterns suitable for each unit space. The smart lighting recognizes each behavior pattern, and controls lighting to suit each unit space and environment. Each test bed has a higher energy saving rate than the conventional LED lighting because the lighting is systematically controlled according to each defined pattern behavior. In particular, lobby, hallway, and stairwells showed energy savings of more than 70% compared to LED lighting, and on average, energy savings of more than 54% (see Figure 4). The scenario based energy saving mechanism in the smart lighting system suggested in this study has high utility for energy saving while providing user convenience.

ACKNOWLEDGMENT

This work was supported by the Technology Innovation Program (10053787, (1) Development of LED system lighting commercializing technologies on unit area based on scalable general purpose lighting devices) funded by the Ministry of Trade, Industry & Energy (Korea).

REFERENCES

[1] J. U. Shin, "The Efficiency of LED lighting using Intelligent Control," The Proceedings of he Korean Institute of IIluminating and Electrical Installation Engineers (KIIEE), vol. 29, no. 1, pp. 4-8, Jan. 2015.

[2] P. Waide, "Phase out of Incandescent lamps," International Energy Agency, Apr. 2010.

[3] J. C. Lee and H. J. Jang, "LED Light Source and Control and Management Lighting System IT Convergence Technology for Energy-saving," The Proceedings of he Korean Institute of IIluminating and Electrical Installation Engineers (KIIEE), vol. 26, no. 1, pp. 15-20, Jan. 2012.

[4] J. Y. Park, J. S. Lee, C. U. Jeong, and E. J. Seo, "A Study on the Visual Point and Preferred Lighting System by Activity in the bedroom," Korean Society for Emotion and Sensibility Fall Conference, pp. 43-44, Nov. 2013.

[5] M. J. Lee, "A Study on the Comparison of the Emotional Experiment from Fluorescent Lamp and LED Lighting" Journal of the Korean Institute of IIluminating and Electrical Installation Engineers, vol.26, no. 8, pp. 8-17, Aug. 2012.

[6] J. H. Kim, J. K. Ko, and M. R. Cho, "A Study of Integrated Evaluation of System Lighting and User Centered Guideline Development-Focused on the Lighting Design Method for Office Space-." Journal of the Korean Institute of Interior Design, vol.23, no. 6, pp. 78-86, Dec. 2014.

CoStack: Collaborative Stack Sharing for Real-Time Embedded Systems

Fabian Mauroner

Institute of Technical Informatics
Graz University of Technology
Graz, Austria
Email: mauroner@tugraz.at

Marcel Baunach

Institute of Technical Informatics
Graz University of Technology
Graz, Austria
Email: baunach@tugraz.at

Abstract—**Embedded real-time systems are targeting for economical stack memory usage and predictable execution flows, what is challenging to unify. In this paper, we propose CoStack, a collaborative stack sharing approach across tasks. CoStack allows defining a collaborative stack memory that can be used by a higher prioritized task if the stack runs out-of-memory. Thus, CoStack virtually reduces the stack memory consumption, leading to a lower memory requirement, and concurrently remains predictable, what is desired for real-time systems. This paper presents an experimental evaluation of CoStack, the synthesized results in a Field Programmable Gate Array (FPGA) and some implementation details of CoStack.**

Keywords–Embedded Systems; Stack handling; Operating-System-Awareness; FPGA implementation

I. INTRODUCTION

Modern real-time embedded systems require, due to their growing complexity and flexibility, evermore memory to fulfill all their challenging requirements. However, embedded system's memory is a restricted resource; thereby, it has to be used in an efficient way.

Global variables are always available for the complete embedded system's life, but local variables are only available and allocated on demand. Therefore, local variables are dynamically allocated on a specific space in the memory, named *stack frame*. The *stack pointer*, indicating the threshold of valid and non-valid data in the stack frame, grows if a local variable is allocated or if Central Processing Unit (CPU) registers are temporally stored (e.g., on function prologue and epilogue). The stack pointer shrinks if the local variables or temporally stored registers are not needed anymore.

In state-of-the-art real-time Operating Systems (OSs) [1][2] for each task an own individual stack frame is allocated; although, it is not fully utilized simultaneously. Therefore, [3][4] show approaches to use a common shared stack frame among all tasks. This reduces the overall stack memory consumption, but restricts the schedulability of all tasks. The reason therefor is that a stack cannot grow if the task's stack pointer is not on the top of the common stack frame. Otherwise, it would destroy data from another task in the common stack frame. Therefore, an individual stack frame is assigned to the tasks in real-time systems by accepting an increasing overall memory consumption. The reason therefor is, for real-time systems, the schedulability and satisfaction of real-time constraints is an essential requirement. This has to be improved to reduce the required computation power and CPU frequency, to reduce the costs and power of the developed embedded real-time system.

Consequently, both, efficient stack memory and schedulability must be unified to improve the memory consumption and to fulfill all the real-time requirements.

Observations showed [5] that not each task fully utilizes its individual stack frame simultaneously, wherefore the approach to share stack memory space among all tasks is used. To avoid the restriction of the schedulability, it must be avoided or at least timely bound that a task is blocked for requesting stack memory. That is possible with the concept of address virtualization [6]. However, this concept requires an additional hardware component, namely the Memory Management Unit (MMU). It translates all Virtual Memory (VM) addresses into Physical Memory (PM) addresses. However, an MMU is only rarely found in embedded systems, because it requires a lot of power and it introduces non-predictable memory accesses. That has to be avoided for real-time systems, which aim for predictability. Therefore, in [7] we presented a dynamic stack sharing approach, which uses VM addresses only for the stack memory and ensures a predictable stack memory access and stack pointer adjustment if the underlying memory architecture behaves predictable, too.

Since the memory is a scarce resource, the software developer has to use it sparsely. However, sometimes it is not possible to optimize the code (e.g., to use an algorithm with less stack memory consumption). Thus, to avoid an out-of-stack, the software developer must guarantee enough stack memory spaces for all tasks at any time. Otherwise, a task would be unpredictably blocked and deadlines may be violated.

A. Related work

In the recent years, there has been done a lot of research to reduce the stack memory consumption, with completely different approaches:

Wang *et al.* proposed the preemptive threshold scheduling in [8], which is used in the ThreadX real-time OS [9]. It is based on Rate Monotonic (RM) scheduling and extends each task with a threshold priority, beyond its nominal priority. If a task is scheduled, its threshold priority is the new priority that must be exceeded to preempt the task by another task's nominal priority. This solution leads to non-preemptive task groups and these are able to use a common shared stack frame. Further, it may improve the schedulability compared to the standard RM scheduling. Nevertheless, sharing the stack memory is not possible between non-preemptive task groups and/or preemptive tasks; thus, sharing the stack memory is limited.

In [10], Chu *et al.* proposed to use a binary translation and a specific kernel by using VM addressed stacks in embedded systems. Thus, their approach allocates only that memory that is required, but the authors showed that for each stack pointer access and adaptation the required run-time is enormous.

Yi *et al.* [11] showed an approach, where a tool analyzes the stack consumption of each task and modifies the developed code on compile time. The modified code calls the *on demand stack* library at each prologue and epilogue of a function. In their use case scenario, the stack memory consumption indeed reduces; however, the execution time increases by $10\,\%$.

Other solutions proposed to allocate the stack memory on the heap. In older works, as for instance [12], on each function prologue and epilogue the heap allocation and deallocation is called, respectively. However, these calls lead to a large run-time overhead for each function.

Works as [13][14] also allocate the stack on the heap. With analyses at compile time, they are able to reduce the large run-time overhead for allocating and deallocating stack memory on the heap. Nevertheless, run-time checks are still required to allocate and deallocate the stack memory.

Middha *et al.* [5] propose to allocate an individual stack frame to each task. If a task overflows (i.e., out-of-stack) its individual stack frame, their approach allocates unused stack memory in another task's individual stack frame. Without code optimization, their run-time consumption increases by around $23\,\%$; with an optimization about $3\,\%$. However, the optimized solution restricts programming features as function pointers and recursive functions.

None of the mentioned works is able to free stack memory voluntarily for a higher prioritized task if no stack memory is available. In [15], Baunach proposed CoMem that is a collaborative memory management in the heap memory for dynamic memory. There, each memory block (in the heap) is handled as a system resource. If a task requests the memory block and is used by another lower prioritized task, the lower prioritized task will be informed. That task has then the control to free the memory block or not.

CoMem enables a collaborative usage of memory blocks in the heap but not for the stack memory. Therefore, in this paper we present *CoStack*, a collaborative stack sharing concept based on a hardware extension, which enables the reduction of the whole stack memory consumption by defining parts in the source code in which the stack memory is collaborative. With the state-of-the-art approaches, there is no possibility to give a higher prioritized task the advantage to use the stack memory instead of a lower prioritized task that owns collaborative stack memory that might voluntarily be released. CoStack ensures the allocation of the required stack memory for higher prioritized tasks by freeing collaborative stack memory from lower prioritized tasks if an out-of-stack condition would result. CoStack does not require a code analysis at compile time; therefore, it is possible to use our approach also in highly dynamic environments, as the Internet of Things (IoT), Industry 4.0, or automotive applications.

The rest of the paper is organized as follows: First, Section II describes in detail the fundamentals of CoStack. Second, Section III analyses the memory improvement and shows the schedulability analysis. Next, Section IV demonstrates implementation aspects in our development platform. Section V shows the CoStack evaluation with an example and the synthesized results for a Field Programmable Gate Array (FPGA). Last, we summarize this work in Section VI.

II. Collaborative Stack Sharing

The collaborative stack sharing approach is based on StackMMU presented in [7]. First, we introduce the terminology and the system assumption. Second, we introduce the fundamentals of StackMMU. Third, we show the extension of the basic StackMMU, which is needed for providing the required information to the hardware. Last, the collaborative stack sharing approach, CoStack, is described in detail.

A. Terminology and Assumption

For CoStack we assume a Reduced Instruction Set Computer (RISC) load/store single-core CPU with Control Status Registers (CSRs), which are CPU registers accessible by specific instructions. Further, we define a multi-tasking system with $\tau \in T$ as a task in the set of tasks T. For each task τ we define, the priority p_τ, the Worst Case Execution Time (WCET) with C_τ defining the time executing on the CPU, and the period or minimum interarrival time with T_τ for periodic or sporadic tasks, respectively. The longest time, in which a priority inversion [16] occurs (i.e., a lower prioritized task runs instead of a higher prioritized task) is denoted as the blocking time B_τ of task τ. Further, we assume that the context switch in the OS and the OS itself consumes no computation time. The stack usage $\sigma_\tau(t) \in \mathbb{N}_0$ defines the stack memory consumption of task τ at time $t \in \mathbb{N}_0$, what can be analyzed with static code analyzers.

B. StackMMU

The StackMMU [7] uses VM addresses for the stack memory. Thus, each task's stack pointer points to a virtual address and StackMMU translates that address to a PM address. For that, the memory is divided into a common area and into a stack area, as depicted in Figure 1. In the common area,

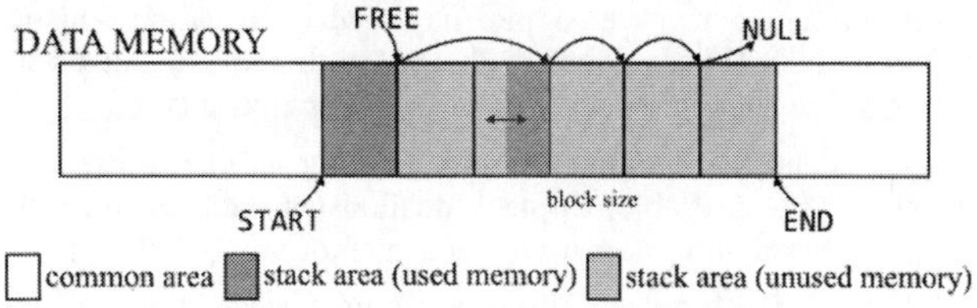

Figure 1. Memory layout of the StackMMU.

all the global data of a task is stored and accessed by PM addresses. The memory for the stack is located, in the stack area. Thereby, the stack area is again divided into blocks, called *pages*. Each page has the same size and is configurable including the start and end of the whole stack area at startup. A linked list contains all available pages, whereby the `FREE` register points to the first free available page. Thus, if a task requires more stack memory and exceeds the available memory in the last appended page, the StackMMU assigns a new page to that task. Thereby, the hardware uses the register `FREE` and updates the Task Control Block (TCB) of the task with the address of the new allocated page. On a stack memory access, first, the hardware reads the PM base address in the

TCB; and second, it accesses the content in the stack area. If the stack page is not required anymore, the hardware frees the page and updates all the required pointers (i.e., `FREE` and the pointer to the next free page in the page). Before a specific stack operation (i.e., growth, access, or shrinkage) is executed, all three operations are performing a read memory operation leading to an additional memory access. However, if the memory access is deterministic, as in many embedded systems, the whole stack operation is also executed in a predictable time as desired for real-time systems.

C. MultiStackMMU

StackMMU restricts the size of the stack pointer change for growing and shrinking in one instruction to the size of a stack page. That limitation is handled by a modified compiler. However, we purged that limitation with MultiStackMMU.

Here, if a stack grows or shrinks more than one page, the hardware extension performs the assignment or deassigment of pages one after another, respectively. This leads to a longer run-time to perform these operations; nevertheless, the execution time remains predictable if the memory accesses itself are deterministic.

Through this extension, the modified compiler, which limited the stack pointer change to one stack page size, is not required anymore. Besides, the hardware is now aware of the number of required pages on a stack memory request, necessary for performing our collaborative stack sharing approach CoStack.

D. CoStack

As long as in the stack area are available more unused pages than required by a task, the pages are properly assigned to the task by the MultiStackMMU approach. However, if there are not enough available pages, an out-of-stack condition occurs. An out-of-stack condition is handled by the OS; nevertheless, the task will be unpredictably blocked until stack memory is available. This would lead to a reduction of the system performance and may lead to real-time constraint violations. Thus, to reduce the possibility of an out-of-stack condition, enough stack memory must be provided.

Instead of blocking the task as long as not enough stack memory is available, CoStack deallocates stack memory from tasks that define their used stack memory as collaborative.

If CoStack detects that the required stack memory pages exceed the free available pages, a *collaborate exception* is triggered and the OS must handle it. Thereby, the stack growth is aborted by the hardware and the OS saves the context of the task. After rescheduling that task, the stack growth instruction will be repeated (i.e., the program counter of the stack growth instruction is stored in the TCB). In the exception handler, the OS searches a lower prioritized task that provides collaborative stack memory. Then, the OS modifies the program counter and schedules the collaborative task. The collaborative task frees the collaborative stack memory and yields itself to return to the OS. There, the scheduler selects the highest prioritized runnable task, which may be the same as the previous one. If a task, that requires stack memory, is scheduled and enough unused pages are available, the required pages are assigned to the task. Otherwise, once again a collaborate exception is triggered and the OS iterates through the tasks as before to search a collaborative task. In case that there are no lower prioritized tasks with collaborative stack memory, the OS has to define a handling strategy to handle this failure as in standard out-of-stack approaches.

Figure 2c demonstrates how a code part can be tagged with collaborative stack. The macros in Figure 2a, Figure 2b, and Figure 2d generate the code for handling CoStack properly. Additionally to the tagged code, which uses a collaborative stack memory, a handler is defined. The handler is only executed if the collaborative stack memory was deallocated for performing some clean-up work, similar to the catch primitive in programming languages such as Java or C++.

Figure 2a shows how the collaborative stack mechanism is performed. First, it checks if the currently running task already defines a collaborative code part. If so, the collaborative code part is already a part of an upper tagged collaborative code part and the `try` part is immediately executed. Otherwise, the handler address and the collaborate frame pointer are stored in the task's TCB. Additionally, the callee saved registers are stored on the stack, to restore them if the collaboration must be performed. Afterwards, the `try` part is executed. If there was no other task requiring the collaborative stack, the callee saved registers on the stack are discarded because the program flow was not manipulated. Otherwise, the program counter continues at the label `COLLABORATE` after a context switch. There, the callee saved registers are restored and the collaborative stack memory space is freed, by using the stored collaborate frame pointer. After that, the collaborate frame pointer in the TCB is cleared and the syscall `yield()` is called for a self-preemption to allow the OS to schedule a higher prioritized task that may wait for stack memory.

III. Analysis

In this section, we analyze the memory utilization of the collaborative stack sharing approach CoStack and compare it with the StackMMU approach. Further, we show the schedulability analysis of CoStack.

A. Memory Consumption

In the StackMMU approach, the stack grows and shrinks with the stack page size $\texttt{page\_size}$. There, the size of the stack changes over time t, depending on the required memory $\sigma_\tau(t)$ by a task τ at time t. Thus, the stack memory consumption of the whole system U is calculated as follows:

$$U(t, \texttt{page\_size}) = \sum_{\tau \in T} \left\lceil \frac{\sigma_\tau(t)}{\texttt{page\_size}} \right\rceil \cdot \texttt{page\_size} \tag{1}$$

Let S denote the totally assigned stack space. To avoid an out-of-stack condition, the stack memory consumption U is not allowed to exceed the totally assigned stack memory S. Otherwise a task would be unpredictably blocked what restricts the schedulability:

$$\forall t \in \mathbb{N}_0 : \quad U(t, \texttt{page\_size}) \leq S \tag{2}$$

With the introduction of the collaborative stack sharing approach, each task τ may define some collaborative stack memory $\kappa_\tau(t)$ at time $t \in \mathbb{N}_0$. This collaborative stack memory κ is available for all higher prioritized tasks, leading

```
  return OS_SUCCESS;
 }

 if(tp->coll_fp == NULL) {
  register uintptr_t *sp asm ("sp");
  uintptr_t *fp = sp;
  tp->handler = &&COLLABORATE;
  tp->coll_fp = fp;
  asm volatile (" addi sp, sp, -48" ::: "sp");
  asm volatile (" sw s0,  -0(%0) \n\t
                  ...
                  sw s11, -44(%0)":: "r" (fp));
  volatile int try_return = try();
  /*here the OS may manipulate the PC to:
    tp->context[CONTEXT_PC] = tp->handler; */
  if(try_return == OS_SUCCESS){
   tp->coll_fp = NULL;
   asm volatile (" addi sp, sp, 48" ::: "sp");
  } else {
  COLLABORATE:
   asm volatile (" lw s0, -0(%0)     \n\t
                   ...
                   lw s11, -44(%0)" :: "r" (fp));
   sp = tp->coll_fp;
   tp->coll_fp = NULL;
   yield();
```

(a) Macro defines the code for handling the collaboration.

```
do {
 __label__ COLLABORATE;
 register os_tcb_t *tp asm ("tp");
 volatile int try(void) {
```

(b) Start of the collaborative stack part macro.

```
int task0(void) {
 while(1) {
  COLLABORATIVE_STACK {
   uint8_t test[600];
   /* other code */
   sleep (TIME_MS(1));
   /* other code */
  } COLLABORATE_STACK {
   /* executed if
      task collaborate */
  } COLLABORATE_STACK_END;
 }
}
```

(c) Task requires a 600 Byte array which memory is tagged as collaborative.

```
  }
 } else
  try();
} while(0);
```

(d) End of the collaborative stack part.

Figure 2. Macros for the collaborative stack sharing approach with a usage example.

to the available collaborative stack pages K_τ at time t for task τ.

$$K_\tau(t) = \sum_{\forall i: p_{\tau_i} < p_\tau} \left\lfloor \frac{\kappa_{\tau_i}(t)}{\texttt{page\_size}} \right\rfloor \cdot \texttt{page\_size} \quad (3)$$

As mentioned in Section II, if a higher prioritized task requires non-available stack memory but collaborative stack memory is available, the collaborative task deallocates its collaborative stack memory to make it available for the higher prioritized task. This means that the stack memory consumption is virtually reduced, leading to the next equation that must be hold to avoid an out-of-stack condition:

$$\forall t \in \mathbb{N}_0, \forall \tau \in T: \quad U(t, \texttt{page\_size}) - K_\tau(t) \leq S \quad (4)$$

Thus, CoStack contributes to the reduction of the totally assigned stack memory S by collaboratively sharing stack memory as shown by comparing the equation (2) with (4).

B. Schedulability Analysis

The freeing of the collaborative stack memory is performed in the respective lower prioritized tasks. Thus, a priority inversion occurs: The lower prioritized task frees the stack memory and blocks the higher prioritized task because the required stack memory is not available. Thus, we are investigating the maximum blocking time B_τ of task τ for the RM schedulability analysis [16]:

$$\frac{C_{\tau_0}}{T_{\tau_0}} + \ldots + \frac{C_{\tau_{n-1}}}{T_{\tau n-1}} + \max\left(\frac{B_{\tau_0}}{T_{\tau_0}}, \ldots, \frac{B_{\tau_{n-1}}}{T_{\tau_{n-1}}}\right) \leq n(2^{\frac{1}{n}} - 1) \quad (5)$$

In CoStack, the blocking time compounds on some administrative work and the freeing of the stack memory. Thereby, the time for freeing the stack memory is not constant, because MultiStackMMU is based on pages, which must be released one after another. Therefore, we are defining the collaborate time $t^k_{\tau\prime}(t)$ of task $\tau\prime$ at time t (see Figure 2a), which defines the time required by the collaborative task $\tau\prime$ to perform all the operations to free $\tau\prime$'s collaborative stack memory. Consequently, the blocking time B_τ of task τ can be calculated as follows:

$$B_\tau := \sum_{\forall i: p_{\tau_i} < p_\tau} \max_{\forall t \in \mathbb{N}} \{t^k_{\tau_i}(t)\} \quad (6)$$

The blocking time B_τ is the sum of the longest collaborate time $t^k_{\tau_i}$ of all lower prioritized tasks τ_i. Thus, the blocking time highly depends on the requested stack memory, the collaborative stack memory of each collaborative task, the number of lower prioritized collaborative tasks, and the time when the stack memory is requested.

IV. Implementation Details

We implemented the collaborative stack sharing approach into our *mosart*MCU research platform, running with the *mosart*MCU-OS.

A. mosartMCU

The *mosart*MCU (i.e., Multi-Core Operating-System-Aware Real-Time MCU) project implements OS awareness into embedded multi-core systems. The open RISC-V [17] architecture, maintained by the University of California of Berkeley, is the specification of the softcore *mosart*MCU. The *mosart*MCU is based on the offered open source Verilog implementation vScale. vScale implements all the 32 Bit integers and the multiplication/division instructions [18] and executes the instruction in a three stage pipeline. The specification specifies 32 registers whereas the compiler does not use the register `tp`. That register indicates the TCB, which contains information about the task including its priority, of the currently running task. We extended the basic implementation with an automatic read operation, triggered by the hardware if the register `tp` is changed. Therefore, the hardware is always aware of the currently running task's priority. In parallel to the normal execution, a read operation is automatically performed by using an additional connection to the data memory through a dual-port memory. This dual-port memory is also used by some other extensions (e.g., [19]). Further, the CPU specification defines three different operating modes, whereas the *mosart*MCU supports only the non-privileged *user*-mode and the privileged *kernel*-mode. These operating modes define permissions for some instructions and for accessing CSRs, which are hardware registers used to configure and to get information from the Microcontroller Unit (MCU).

B. mosartMCU-OS

The *mosart*MCU-OS is a real-time OS supporting the OS-awareness extension of the *mosart*MCU. Besides other OS-awareness concepts, it only has to initialize some CSRs (i.e., stack area) and the references of the next free available pages at startup, for supporting MultiStackMMU. After that, the MultiStackMMU operates transparent to the OS. However, the OS must be extended to support our proposed collaborative stack sharing approach.

C. Collaborative Stack Management

In a CSR, the hardware provides the number of required stack pages after a collaborate exception. The exception handler stores the number of required pages into the TCB of the currently running task. After executing the exception handler, the OS does its management work and selects a task according to the RM scheduling policy. Before leaving the OS, by restoring all the task's registers, the OS checks if the scheduled task requires more pages than available. The number of available pages is provided by the hardware through another CSR register. If there are more pages available than required, the OS lefts and resumes with the scheduled task. Otherwise, the OS searches, starting by the lowest prioritized task, a collaborative task that is recognized by the information in the TCB. If a collaborative task is found, the scheduler selects that task for executing. Thereby, the scheduler changes the program counter to continue at the collaborate handler, also stored in the TCB. The collaborate code restores its callee saved registers, frees the collaborate stack memory, and yields itself to return to the OS.

V. Experimental Evaluation

We experimentally evaluated the collaborative stack sharing approach in the *mosart*MCU, running with 50 MHz in a Xilinx Artix-7 FPGA. First, we demonstrate the cooperative stack sharing, measured with an oscilloscope; and second, we show the synthesized results for the FPGA.

A. CoStack Evaluation

This evaluation illustrates CoStack on a collaborative 600 Byte stack memory provided by task $\tau\prime$, once the stack memory is not available for the higher prioritized task τ. Figure 3 depicts the execution flow with the signal *os* showing

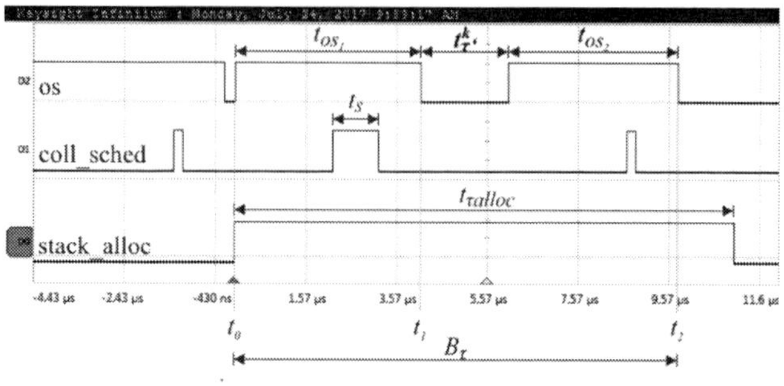

Figure 3. Execution flow example of CoStack.

the execution of the OS, the signal *coll_sched* demonstrating the part in the scheduler that is responsible for searching and scheduling a collaborative task, and the signal *stack_alloc* showing the time for allocating the required 600 Bytes stack memory to task τ. Table I lists all the measured times, and

TABLE I. Measured times for the example in Figure 3.

t_{os_1}	t_s	t_{os_2}	$t^k_{\tau\prime}$	B_τ	$t_{\tau alloc}$
3.74 µs	1.02 µs	4.08 µs	1.94 µs	9.76 µs	11.00 µs

following emphasizes some specific points in time of Figure 3:

- At time t_0, task τ requests 600 Byte stack memory. The memory is not available; therefore, the OS is called by a collaborate exception. There, the OS saves the context of task τ, does its management work including the work for scheduling the collaborative task $\tau\prime$ (i.e., t_s), and restores its context. All this in total consumes t_{os_1}.
- At time t_1, the OS returns, and task $\tau\prime$ is running. Instead of continuing with the previous preempted program counter it continues at the label `COLLABORATE`. There, its callee saved registers are restored, the collaborative stack memory $\kappa_{\tau\prime}$ is released, and the task yields to return to the OS, which again schedules task τ. These operations reflect the collaborate time $t^k_{\tau\prime}$.
- After leaving the OS (i.e., t_{OS_2}) on time t_2, there is enough stack memory available for task τ; therefore, the required stack memory is allocated to task τ.

The blocking time B_τ (i.e., $t^k_{\tau\prime}$ including the OS overheads t_{OS_1} and t_{OS_2}) and the stack allocation time $t_{\tau alloc}$ are not constant, because they depend on the number of collaborative tasks, the location of the task in the searching list, and the number of required and collaborate stack pages. However, the execution is still predictable because MultiStackMMU works predictable. Further, CoStack avoids an out-of-stack, because the collaborative task $\tau\prime$ voluntarily frees its collaborative stack memory $\kappa_{\tau\prime}$ for the higher prioritized task τ. Otherwise, task τ would not be able to execute, because no stack memory is

TABLE II. Resource comparison of the original and the extended *mosart*MCU.

	*mosart*MCU		
	Original	MultiStackMMU	CoStack
LUT slices	2799	4283	4298
FF slices	2078	2378	2378
max. frequency	73.992 MHz	63.339 MHz	63.391 MHz
Dynamic power	16 mW	21 mW	21 mW

available; consequently, this might result into an unpredictable blocking of task τ and to possibly violated real-time constraints.

B. Synthesized Results

The synthesized results, provided by the Xilinx Vivado 2017.3 development toolchain, for the Xilinx Artix-7 FPGA are listed in Table II. It compares Look Up Table (LUT) slices, Flip-Flop (FF) slices, the maximum achievable frequency, and the dynamic power of the original *mosart*MCU, and the extended versions MultiStackMMU and CoStack. If we compare the original *mosart*MCU with the extended versions, it is remarkable that the original version requires about 65 % and 87 % of LUTs and FFs, respectively. The increased resource utilization is caused by the VM address translation and some other registers that are required for handling the StackMMU approach. However, comparing the two extended *mosart*MCU versions, the resource utilization remains negligible the same.

For the maximal achievable frequency, and the dynamic power consumption the table represents a similar behavior. For the former, the large frequency reduction is caused by the implementation of the StackMMU in the already longest path of the original *mosart*MCU. For the latter, the dynamic power increases due to the additional required LUTs and FFs. However, for the two extended *mosart*MCU versions, the maximum achievable frequency remains almost the same and both require the same amount of power.

VI. Conclusion

Memory is a rare and expensive resource in embedded systems. This makes the economical usage of memory important. The stack memory has the potential to optimize the overall memory consumption because its size changes dynamically over the time. The paper proposes CoStack, an extension of the dynamically sharing stack memory concept StackMMU with collaborative stack memory. A task tags a code part with collaborative stack memory and if a higher prioritized task requires stack memory that is not available at that moment, the collaborative task deallocates the collaborative stack memory for enabling the higher prioritized task to continue. Our analysis shows that the whole stack memory requirement is virtually reduced. Further, we showed the impact of CoStack in the schedulability analysis for RM scheduling. The experimental evaluation shows that the synthesized results for the FPGA remain almost constant. Therefore, CoStack contributes to a reduction of the memory usage by introducing a collaborative stack sharing mechanism and remains predictable as aimed for real-time systems.

Acknowledgment

This research project was partially funded by AVL List GmbH and the Austrian Federal Ministry of Sciences, Research and Economy (bmwfw).

References

[1] "Micrium uC/OS-III," URL: https://www.micrium.com/rtos/ [accessed: 2018-02-27].

[2] "The FreeRTOS Kernel," URL: http://www.freertos.org/ [accessed: 2018-02-27].

[3] "Contiki: The Open Source OS for the Internet of Things," URL: http://www.contiki-os.org [accessed: 2018-02-27].

[4] T. P. Baker, "A stack-based resource allocation policy for realtime processes," in Proc. of the 11th IEEE Real-Time Systems Symposium (RTSS), Dec 1990, pp. 191–200.

[5] B. Middha, M. Simpson, and R. Barua, "MTSS: Multitask Stack Sharing for Embedded Systems," ACM Trans. on Embedded Computer Systems, vol. 7, 2008, pp. 41:1–46:37, ISSN: 0001-0782.

[6] J. Fotheringham, "Dynamic Storage Allocation in the Atlas Computer, Including an Automatic Use of a Backing Store," Communications of the ACM, vol. 4, 1961, pp. 435–436, ISSN: 0001-0782.

[7] F. Mauroner and M. Baunach, "StackMMU: Dynamic Stack Sharing for Embedded Systems," in Proc. of the 22nd IEEE Int. Conference on Emerging Technologies and Factory Automation (ETFA), Sep 2017, pp. 1–9.

[8] Y. Wang and M. Saksena, "Scheduling Fixed-Priority Tasks with Preemption Threshold," in Proc. of the 6th Int. Conference on Real-Time Computing Systems and Applications (RTCSA), 1999, pp. 328–335.

[9] "ThreadX," 2018, URL: https://rtos.com/solutions/threadx/real-time-operating-system/ [accessed: 2018-02-27].

[10] R. Chu, L. Gu, Y. Liu, M. Li, and X. Lu, "SenSmart: Adaptive Stack Management for Multitasking Sensor Networks," IEEE Trans. on Computers, vol. 62, 2013, pp. 137–150, ISSN: 0018-9340.

[11] S. Yi, S. Lee, Y. Cho, and J. Hong, OTL: On-Demand Thread Stack Allocation Scheme for Real-Time Sensor Operating Systems. Springer Berlin Heidelberg, 2007, pp. 905–912, in Computational Science – ICCS 2007, ISBN: 978-3-540-72590-9.

[12] E. A. Hauck and B. A. Dent, "Burroughs' B6500/B7500 Stack Mechanism," in Proc. of the Spring Joint Computer Conference, ser. AFIPS '68 (Spring), 1968, pp. 245–251.

[13] D. Grunwald and R. Neves, "Whole-program Optimization for Time and Space Efficient Threads," in Proc. of the 7th Int. Conference on Architectural Support for Programming Languages and Operating Systems (ASPLOS), ser. ASPLOS VII, 1996, pp. 50–59.

[14] R. von Behren, J. Condit, F. Zhou, G. C. Necula, and E. Brewer, "Capriccio: Scalable Threads for Internet Services," in Proc. of the 9th ACM Symposium on Operating Systems Principles (SOSP), ser. SOSP '03, 2003, pp. 268–281.

[15] M. Baunach, "CoMem: collaborative memory management for real-time operation within reactive sensor/actor networks," Trans. on Real-Time Systems, vol. 48, 2012, pp. 75–100, ISSN: 1573-1383.

[16] L. Sha, R. Rajkumar, and J. P. Lehoczky, "Priority Inheritance Protocols: An Approach to Real-Time Synchronization," IEEE Trans. on Computers, vol. 39, Sep 1990, pp. 1175–1185, ISSN: 0018-9340.

[17] "RISC-V," URL: https://riscv.org/ [accessed: 2018-02-27].

[18] A. Waterman, Y. Lee, R. Avizienis, D. Patterson, and K. Asanovic, The RISC-V Instruction Set Manual, 2016, URL: https://riscv.org/specifications/ [accessed: 2018-02-27].

[19] F. Mauroner and M. Baunach, "EventIRQ: An Event based and Priority aware IRQ handling for Multi-Tasking Environments," in Proc. of the 20th Euromicro Conference on Digital System Design (DSD), Aug 2017, pp. 102–110.

PACER

Peripheral Activity Completion Estimation and Recognition

Daniel Ross Moore
Center for Efficient, Scalable and Reliable Computing
Dept. of Electrical and Computer Engineering
North Carolina State University, Raleigh, USA
e-mail: drmoore2@ncsu.edu

Alexander G. Dean
Center for Efficient, Scalable and Reliable Computing
Dept. of Electrical and Computer Engineering
North Carolina State University, Raleigh, USA
e-mail: agdean@ncsu.edu

Abstract—**Embedded peripheral devices such as memories, sensors and communications interfaces are used to perform a function external to a host microcontroller. The device manufacturer typically specifies worst-case current consumption and latency estimates for each of these peripheral actions. Peripheral Activity Completion, Estimation and Recognition (PACER) is introduced as a suite of algorithms that can be applied to detect completed peripheral operations in real-time. By detecting activity completion, PACER enables the host to exploit slack between the worst-case estimate and the actual response time. These methods were tested independently and in conjunction with IODVS on multiple common peripheral devices. For the peripheral devices under test, the test fixture confirmed decreases in energy expenditures of up to 80% and latency reductions of up to 67%.**

Keywords-embedded systems; energy aware embedded computing; embedded profiling; embedded performance analysis; Dynamic Voltage Scaling (DVS); low-power; low-energy; wireless sensor node (WSN); adaptive embedded systems.

I. INTRODUCTION

Embedded systems are often constrained by timing and energy budgets because both factors affect the resultant cost and size of the system. Peripheral devices external to the microcontroller (MCU) such as those shown in Figure 1 can play a significant role in system-wide energy consumption. There are many methods available for decreasing the static power usage of peripherals [1] [2] [3]. PACER decreases dynamic power consumption and latency by exploiting the slack between actual versus worst-case operation time.

Device manufacturers derive and specify the worst-case operation duration by summing exacerbating factors including age, temperature and voltage. Using the worst-case operation time as a naïve guideline, the worst-case energy consumption of a given operation is characterized by (1).

$$E_{op-wc} = \int_{0}^{t_{op}} P_{op}(t)dt + \int_{t_{op}}^{t_{slack}} P_{slack}(t)dt \qquad (1)$$

Where t_{op} and P_{op} are the time and power comprising the actual operation while t_{slack} and P_{slack} are the time and power comprising the period between operation completion and the worst-case execution time.

Most peripheral devices provide a mechanism for signaling that operations completed earlier than the maximum. However, using these mechanisms results in sub-optimal power performance. For example, a common method of detecting write completion on external non-volatile memory relies on polling a status register. Performing this signaled method has power and energy consequences:

$$P_{overhead} = P_{MCU} + P_{MCD} + P_{Comm} + P_{Match} + P_{Dev} \qquad (2)$$

- P_{MCU}: MCU must be active while polling
- P_{MCD}: MCU communications driver must be active
- P_{Comm}: Communications incurs $P = cfV_{dd}^{2}$ penalty
- P_{Match}: MCU and device voltages must be matched.
  - Neither can use dynamic voltage scaling
- P_{Dev}: Device communications driver must be active

$$E_{op-sig} = \int_{0}^{t_{op}} \left(P_{op}(t) + P_{overhead}(t)\right)dt \qquad (3)$$

The components of $P_{overhead}$ are highly variable between microcontrollers, systems and devices. The signal may involve protocol-level communication or it may be as simple as an interrupt pin and that signal may traverse PCB traces with considerable capacitance. E_{op-sig} can exceed E_{op-wc}.

Both interface methods incur a power penalty and the naïve worst-case method also incurs a latency penalty. As the energy cost of computation continues to decrease in modern microcontrollers, it becomes more rewarding to use onboard intelligence to minimize the impact of power and latency penalties. PACER develops adaptive timing, current usage and charge consumption heuristics for estimating or recognizing early completion of peripheral operations, thus reducing total latency and energy consumption.

The prediction is verified in real-time against the actual state and the heuristic is updated with the results. In this fashion, the algorithms are resistant to variations in behavior that may occur across the lifecycle of the device. PACER is evaluated against a variety of embedded peripherals and is

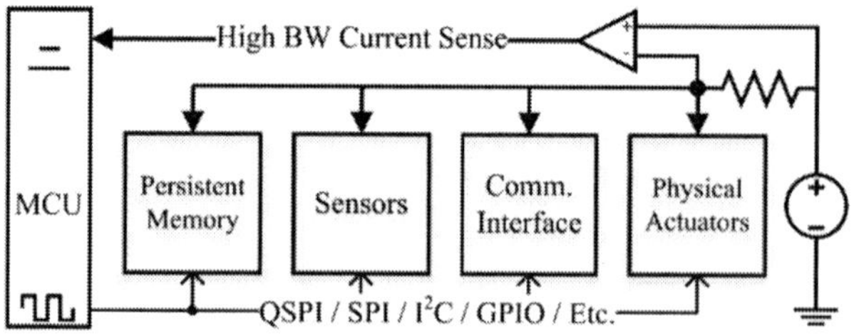

Figure 1: Typical Embedded System with Device Current Feedback

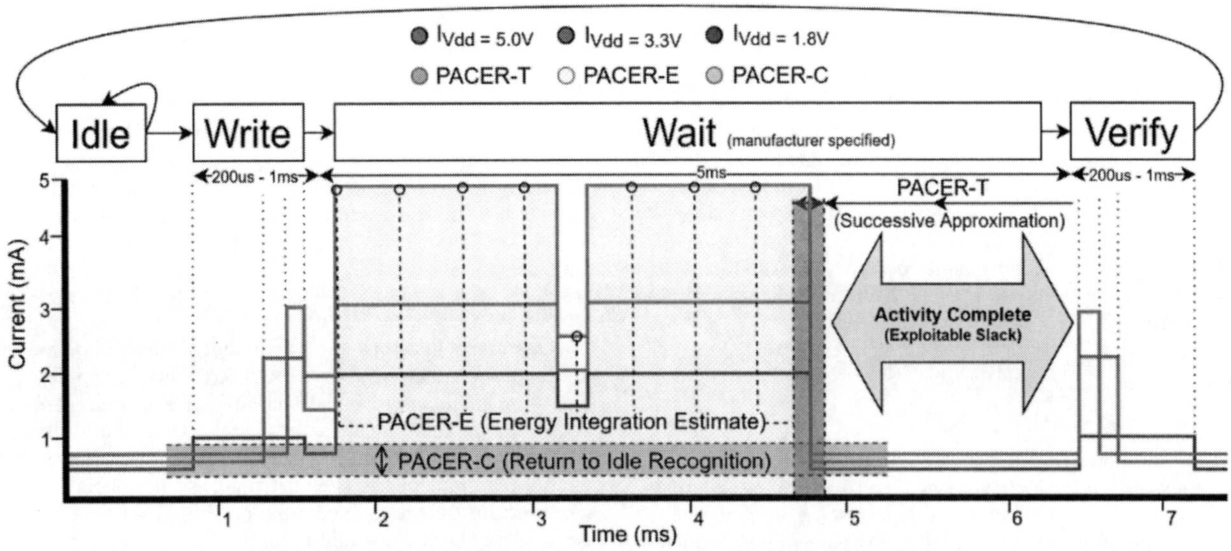

Figure 2: A Typical External Memory Transaction with IODVS and PACER

shown to significantly decrease both energy consumption and latency of peripherals with minimal computational overhead.

Figure 2 shows the current profile for the common peripheral operation of writing a page to EEPROM. The manufacturer-specified mandatory wait period is 5ms, beginning about the 1.75ms mark. As the device transitions through the Idle → Write → Wait → Verify states, it can be inferred from the current profile that the operation completed by the 4.75ms mark and that it was not necessary to delay until approximately 6.5ms per the specification. This 1.75ms differential is slack that can be exploited to decrease latency.

There are a wide variety of peripheral devices with a correspondingly wide variety of completion determinism and current profiles. PACER introduces three methods by which the host MCU can estimate or detect early completion of peripheral operations while also minimizing computational overhead. Devices with highly deterministic timing respond best to the timing heuristic while those with variable timing respond best to current or charge heuristics. Through low-overhead early completion detection, PACER is able to decrease both latency and system-wide energy consumption.

II. Related Work

Intra-Operation Dynamic Voltage Scaling [4] (IODVS) has been shown to significantly reduce the energy consumption of embedded peripherals (Flash, EEPROM, sensors, etc.) during their voltage-independent states. These states typically occur during mandatory delay periods while the peripheral completes a specified operation. When implementing IODVS, the host MCU and peripheral devices are placed on different voltage domains throughout the course of the voltage-independent state. Because of this, it is not possible for the MCU to poll the peripheral device for operation completion. Polling is also shown to be a rather costly operation due to (2) and (3). Without the ability to communicate to the peripheral device, PACER is necessary to achieve minimal operation latencies.

A. *Timing Heuristic*

Peripheral operations can vary in their latency or completion times due to a number of factors. Temperature can significantly affect the completion time for peripherals with deterministic timing requirements such as DRAM [5]. Device aging can also affect timing due to a number of issues resulting from fundamental semiconductor physics [6]. Furthermore, some devices simply have non-deterministic completion times due to features such as MMUs and caches that are implemented in various data storage devices like Micro-SD cards, or age and wear as they effect FLASH storage timing.

Because the latency can vary significantly between operations, it is necessary to develop a timing heuristic that can adapt to slowly changing effects like age and temperature as well as rapidly changing factors like cache hits and misses. Adaptive delay estimation is not a new problem [7] and research continues to compensate for non-deterministic delay with different approaches for wireless communications, control systems and mass storage latency [8].

B. *Energy Heuristic*

For devices with highly variable timing and dynamic current consumption characteristics, integrating the current consumption of the device throughout an operation can allow for better detection of completion. Some operations can be characterized by the amount of charge necessary to complete them. This technique is referred to as "coulomb counting" and is a common technique used to determine the state of charge in rechargeable batteries [9].

C. *Current Heuristic*

The completion of some peripheral operations are easily detectable by their current consumption profile. These devices have a distinct and deterministic current profile that can be characterized and used to estimate the moment when an operation completes.

Simple and differential power analysis (SPA and DPA) attacks are performed by monitoring device current consumption with very fine grained detail. These attacks seek to undermine encryption techniques by monitoring the current consumption of the processor and detecting the moment at which the processor executes a branch operation [10]. The attacks have been performed on an ARM Cortex MCU using AES and required an extensive measurement setup to accomplish [11]. PACER is inspired by this previous work using fine-grained in-circuit current measurement and fortunately benefits from much more lenient sampling requirements.

III. METHODS

A. Timing Heuristic PACER-T

Some peripheral operations exhibit highly deterministic timing qualities. Such a device is likely to be internally clocked and the operation is waiting for some number of clock cycles to expire before signaling that the operation completed. Such operations are typified Figure 3 in that neither the total energy consumed, nor the profile of that consumption are necessary to predict completion. Regardless of the power profile, the operation always completes within a narrow window of time. Erases and write operations to EEPROM and flash are typical examples of this behavior.

PACER-T uses the successive approximation algorithm shown in (4) to determine the optimal delay for an operation. The algorithm begins by executing an operation with the amount of delay specified in the device datasheet. After each iteration, if the operation completed earlier than predicted (Pass), then the amount of delay is halved. Otherwise, the operation was ongoing (Fail) and the next delay is increased by half the distance to the last previously successful operation.

$$\begin{aligned} Pass&: \begin{cases} T_{upper} = T_{lower} \\ T_{lower} = T_{lower} - \dfrac{(T_{upper} - T_{lower})}{2} \end{cases} \\ Fail&: \left\{ T_{lower} = T_{lower} + \dfrac{(T_{upper} - T_{lower})}{2} \right. \\ &Initial\ Conditions: T_{upper} = T_{worst-case}, T_{lower} = 0 \end{aligned} \tag{4}$$

The algorithm is executed online and provides the tightest possible timing. Upon expiration of the predicted wait period, if the device status register indicates that the operation is still occurring, then the algorithm has yielded an early prediction and it is appropriate to continue to wait. This would be considered the 'Fail' case of (4) and future estimates are increased. Otherwise, if the device status register indicates that the operation is complete, then the algorithm has yielded a late prediction and it is appropriate to reduce future estimates.

B. Energy Heuristic PACER-E

Operations that consume a deterministic amount of energy are better characterized by PACER-E. For example, the operation might involve the charging of a storage element such as an inductor or capacitor. In any case, a certain amount of energy is required to complete the operation and once that energy requirement has been satisfied, the peripheral device considers the operation to be complete. Figure 4 is an example of an energy bound operation.

The energy based heuristic was performed similarly to PACER-T in that successive approximation is used. The system multiply-accumulates voltage and current samples fed to the peripheral device. When the digital integration has reached the test value, the operation is 'complete' and checked for correctness. The mechanics of (4) are applied to PACER-E, except that all T limits are replaced with E energy limits. PACER-E is slightly less precise than the timing based algorithm due to the time required to both sample and perform the digital integration necessary for threshold checking.

The energy consumed throughout a test is calculated using the fundamental relationship shown in (5). The results were calculated offline via (6) and (7), where S is the state of the device, and T_s is the sampling period.

$$P = VI = \frac{E}{t} \tag{5}$$

$$E_s = \sum_{n=0}^{N-1} V_n I_n T_s \tag{6}$$

$$E_{total} = \sum_{S_0}^{S_{n-1}} E_s \tag{7}$$

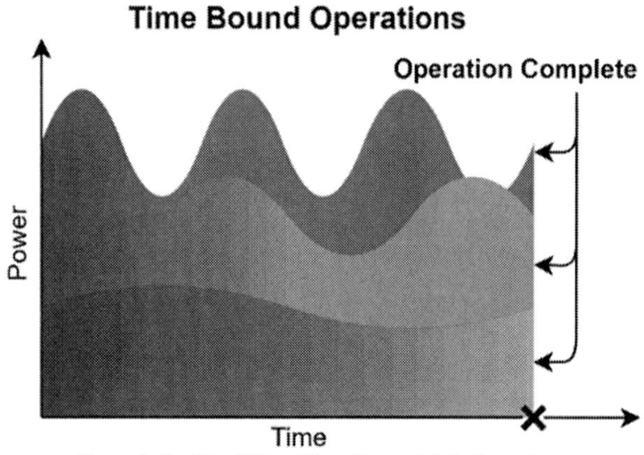

Figure 3: Profile of Three Time-Deterministic Operations

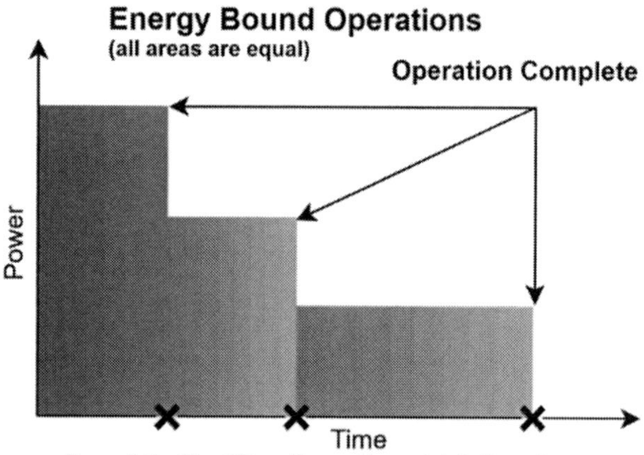

Figure 4: Profile of Three Energy-Deterministic Operations

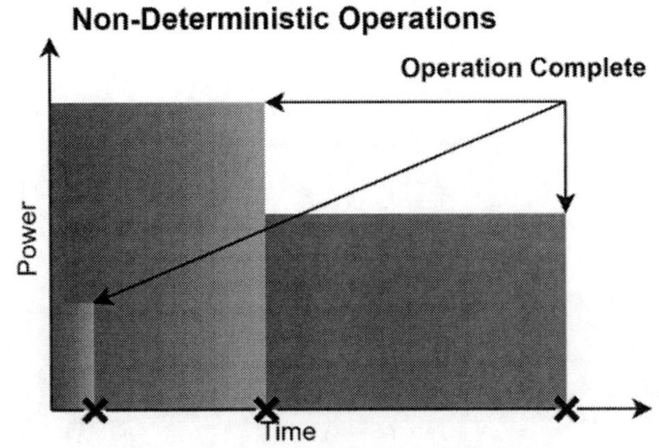

Figure 5: Profile of Three Non-Deterministic Operations

C. *Current Heuristic PACER-C*

Some operations cannot reliably be defined in terms of time nor energy. One example of a non-deterministic operation would be communications tasks performed by Ethernet or wireless devices that have non-deterministic transmission latencies. Another example would be memory devices that incorporate an onboard memory hierarchy. In such devices, operations are affected by cache latencies.

PACER-C provides recognition that the operation is complete by measuring the idle current usage of the device before the operation begins and marking the operation as complete after the current returns to idle. In order to accommodate operations where the current returns to idle and yet the operation has not yet completed, the algorithm incorporates both a minimum latency and an idle current percent threshold to mark the operation as complete.

Algorithm 1: *PACER-C*

```
ICT = (Idle Current Measurement) * threshold
Execute Peripheral Device Operation
While (t < Minimum Latency) and (I > ICT) then
    I = New Current Measurement
End While
```

PACER-C is described by Algorithm 1 and begins by taking a sample of the device input current while idle. Next, the operation is executed and the algorithm waits for a minimum latency period to expire. The operation is considered complete after the output current returns to the threshold percentage of its previous state. The threshold for all following experiments was set empirically at 110%.

PACER-C is the most basic method to determine in real time if an operation is complete and may also be prone to false positives in some cases. There are many more advanced algorithms that can suit the purpose such as a multi-layer perceptron that is used in neural networks that could be used to identify features in real-time. It is notable however, that reducing the complexity of the detector is important so that the algorithm can ensure that it is keeping pace with incoming samples. Naturally, more complex algorithms could be accommodated by a more powerful host microcontroller.

IV. MATERIALS

PACER and IODVS are implemented on an STM32F429 MCU supported by the STMicroelectronics DISCO board and hosted by the PRIME (Precise Real-Time In-Circuit Micro-EMS) assembly. The board provides 64MB of SDRAM which allows for simultaneous sampling throughout the test suite at very high speed. All experiments were sampled at 1MSPS and the SDRAM allowed any individual experiment to last up to 1 full second. All of the analog conversions as well as the device state sampling were performed via DMA. Therefore, the test fixture is expected to have had no impact on the operation under test.

The PRIME assembly, shown in Figure 6, hosts a variety of peripherals (labelled in red as DUT: Devices Under Test) that are common in embedded designs. The board provides access to Bluetooth, Wi-Fi and a Si1143 proximity detector. PACER was evaluated on NAND and NOR FLASH memories, as well as a commercial EEPROM, temperature / humidity sensor and four independent Micro-SD cards.

At 1 MSPS and 4 channel measurements and 2 bytes per sample, each test can result in up to 8 megabytes of data. Because repeatability is so important, each test was run 50 times. Therefore, bandwidth became a limiting factor and a Hi-Speed (480Mbps) USB module was added to the board to allow for rapid development. Operating as a virtual communications port and using MCU parallel bus, actual bandwidth was realized at approximately 120Mbps.

Each of the peripheral devices under test has some method of determining if an operation completed successfully. For the memory devices, a simple read-back verification is sufficient to determine correctness and is a common practice among embedded designs. The temperature and humidity sensor provides a status bit indicating if an operation is in progress, thus indicating that a requested operation has not yet completed.

Power is provided and voltage is modulated to each individual device on the domain using independently configurable power supplies. The ASDM-300F module shown in orange on Figure 6 provides a high-efficiency buck power supply, followed by a linear regulator with a high ripple-rejection ratio. A high-precision and clean power

Figure 6: PRIME (Precise Real-Time In-Circuit Micro-EMS)

supply is important because PACER uses the current profile to make real-time decisions. If the power supply outputs a significant amount of noise, then it becomes difficult to acquire signal and determine activity completion in real-time.

The ASDM-300F is also outfitted with a dual current measurement circuit using the Maxim MAX4377HAUA+. This circuit allows the host to measure both the input and output current of the power supply with high analog bandwidth. Ultimately, these outputs are used to determine activity completion with the PACER-E and PACER-C algorithms. It is important to note the gain-bandwidth product of the amplifier. High frequency content will be attenuated to some degree and the actionable data output would be of higher quality if a higher frequency device were available.

While measuring and classifying activity completion, it is important that each device be analyzed independently. The PPS-330D shown in yellow on Figure 6 allows the host to switch the voltage domain of an individual peripheral to any one of three domains, or disconnect the device entirely

PPS-330D devices are connected to each peripheral, and while a peripheral is under test, the remaining devices are switched to an alternate voltage domain. Thus, each device is independently classified in-system without physically removing other devices that may affect current measurements. Once the devices are characterized, then their individual contributions to the power supply current output can be deduced through superposition. The PPS-330D is convenient for initial profiling, but unnecessary for a streamlined implementation. The ASDM-300F is necessary for an IODVS implementation, but PACER-E and PACER-C only require the current measurement component.

V. Results

Initial IODVS results were repeated so as to establish a baseline with which to compare the results of PACER. Previous experiments required the results to be averaged many times over. The PRIME assembly provides high enough signal to noise ratio that averaging multiple test results is unnecessary and a simple 50-sample moving average provides enough filtering while maintaining a quick response time.

A. MCP25AA512 EEPROM

The Microchip EEPROM is specified by the manufacturer for a 5ms mandatory wait period following the write command and data. This operation is highly deterministic with respect to time, energy and current profile. All PACER algorithms identified activity completion with high accuracy.

TABLE I. MCP25AA512 EEPROM PACER Results

Stage	Latency Results (ms)				
	Control	*PACER-T*	*Diff.*	*PACER+IODVS*	*Diff.*
Wait	5.05	3.51	30.5%	3.51	30.5%
All	5.98	4.44	25.7%	4.44	25.7%
	Energy Results (uJ)				
Wait	46.84	37.89	19.1%	27.85	40.5%
All	53.05	43.91	17.2%	32.40	38.9%

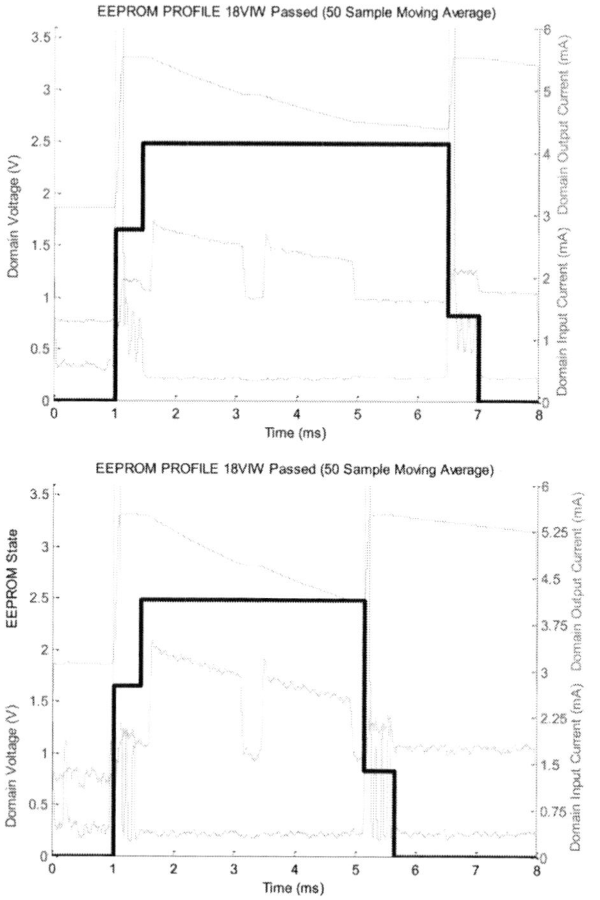

Figure 7: EEPROM Write Cycle Using IODVS and PACER-T

The current waveform of Figure 7 shows that the EEPROM write operation begins at t=1.5ms and indicates completion at approximately t=5ms instead of t=6.5ms as specified by the manufacturer. After applying the PACER-T algorithm, it is indeed true that the operation was complete at the 5ms mark, thus reducing the wait latency by 30.5%.

The PACER-E and PACER-C algorithms were also successful in identifying activity completion. The two algorithms do require additional computation to integrate or otherwise observe the current waveform. Given identical performance, PACER-T is the best choice in this application.

B. Numonyx M25PX16 NOR Serial Flash

NOR flash modules sacrifice byte-wise modification for overall capacity. The M25PX16 presents 16MBits of capacity in a small package, but the host must erase sub-sectors of flash (4K) to write pages of flash (128B). To perform a read-modify-write operation, the host must read the contents of a sub-sector, modify the contents locally, erase the sub-sector in flash and finally write the modified contents back to the flash on a page-by-page basis.

Both the sub-sector erase and page write have a worst-case delay specified by the manufacturer. PACER algorithms were run against both operations to find the comprehensive result.

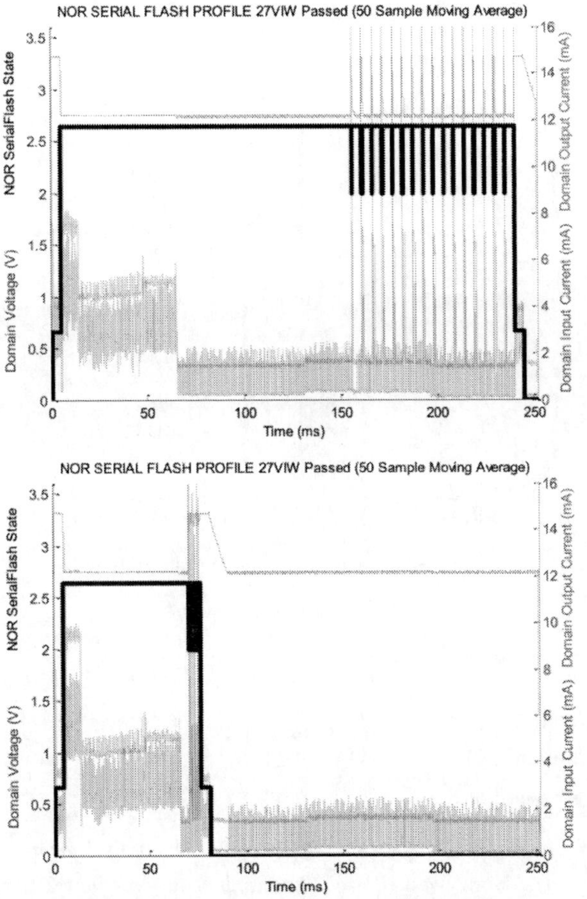

Figure 8: NOR Serial Flash Write-Cycle using IODVS and PACER-T

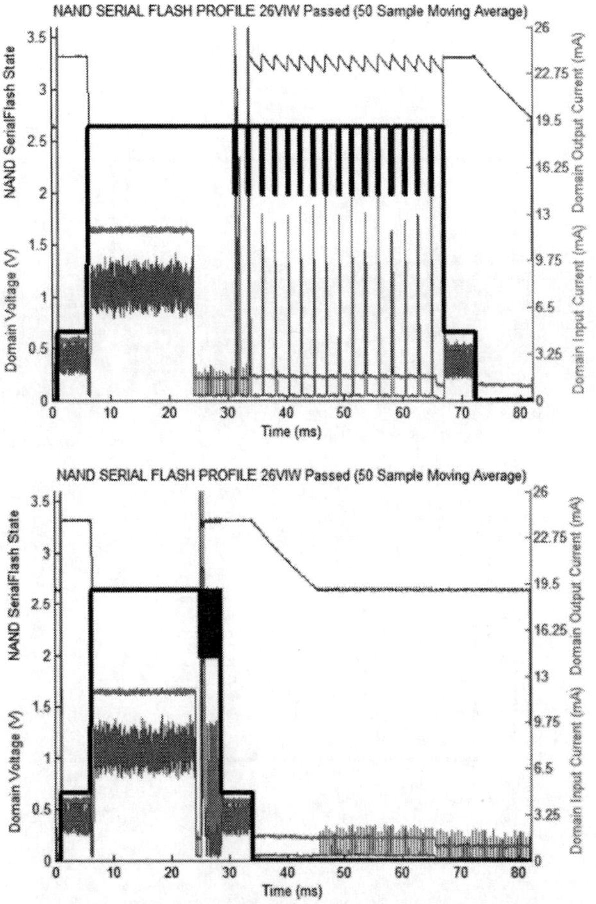

Figure 9: NAND Serial Flash Write Cycle Using IODVS and PACER-T

Although specified for 150ms, the current waveform indicates that the sub-sector erase completed approximately 65ms after it begins. Page writes are specified for a worst-case completion time of 10ms but through the application of PACER-T, they complete much faster as shown in TABLE II. The wait figure is the total amount of time spent waiting for the erase and the aggregate amount of time for each page write. The PACER-T algorithm delivered a 70% decrease in wait latency which yielded a 38.9% decrease in overall energy consumption. The worst-case manufacturer specification appears to be very pessimistic, although may be appropriate across both process and temperature variables.

TABLE II. M25PX16 NOR SERIAL FLASH PACER RESULTS

Stage	Latency Results (ms)				
	Control	*PACER-T*	*Diff.*	*PACER+IODVS*	*Diff.*
Wait	231.57	69.47	70.0%	66.92	71.1%
All	243.87	82.45	66.2%	80.26	67.1%
	Energy Results (uJ)				
Wait	2138.3	1212.0	43.3%	1029.52	51.9%
All	2277.0	1392.0	38.9%	1158.26	49.1%

C. *Microchip SST26VF016B Serial NAND Flash*

The SST26 serial flash module uses NAND-like control logic to provide higher capacity and lower latency than the NOR serial flash. However, the device sacrifices the random-access timing benefit of NOR flash. The serial flash module must therefore read an entire page of flash into a local buffer before providing read data to the host. This can result in non-deterministic read and write access times.

While the core logic differs from the M25PX16, the PACER-T algorithm still performed the best. Application yielded a 66.6% decrease in aggregate wait times and a 17.8% decrease in overall energy consumption.

TABLE III. SST26VF016B NAND SERIAL FLASH PACER RESULTS

Stage	Latency Results (ms)				
	Control	*PACER-T*	*Diff.*	*PACER+IODVS*	*Diff.*
Wait	57.61	19.26	66.6%	19.27	66.6%
All	71.28	32.94	53.8%	32.95	53.8%
	Energy Results (uJ)				
Wait	1053.0	806.2	23.8%	584.87	44.5%
All	1247.9	997.26	17.8%	801.95	35.7%

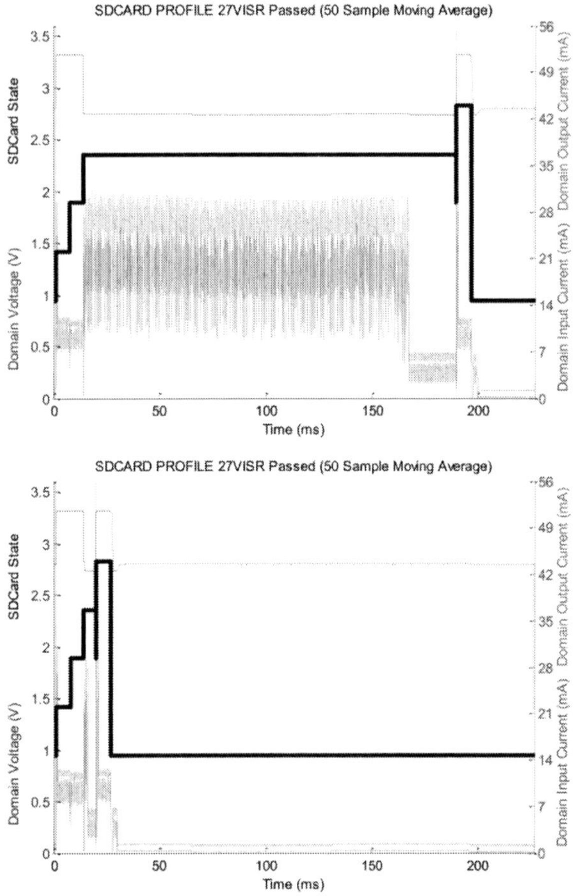

Figure 10: A Micro-SD Card Cache Miss and a Cache Hit

D. *An assortment of Micro-SD Memory Cards*

Onboard caches and memory management units cause the write operation of Micro-SD cards to have non-deterministic timing. In this case, PACER-C is the only algorithm that can reliably detect when the operation is finished. As with all memory tests, writes were performed with random data to random addresses throughout the memory space and so the cache performance is thoroughly exercised. Figure 10 shows the massive power and latency difference between a cache miss and a cache hit.

Figure 11 helps to describe the performance differences shown in TABLE IV. The control delay is set to the median delay for each characterization, PACER-C allows the host to react to those operations deviating considerably from the median. Therefore, the Sandisk and Lexar cards benefitted considerably because they exhibit a bimodal timing distribution. The Swissbit card benefits decisively because of the mostly normal timing distribution. The Kingston card does not benefit as much because write timing exhibits a very low standard deviation. To present complete timing effects, a thorough latency analysis would need to be done on each device. Only energy results are presented here, but they are correlated with overall latency decreases.

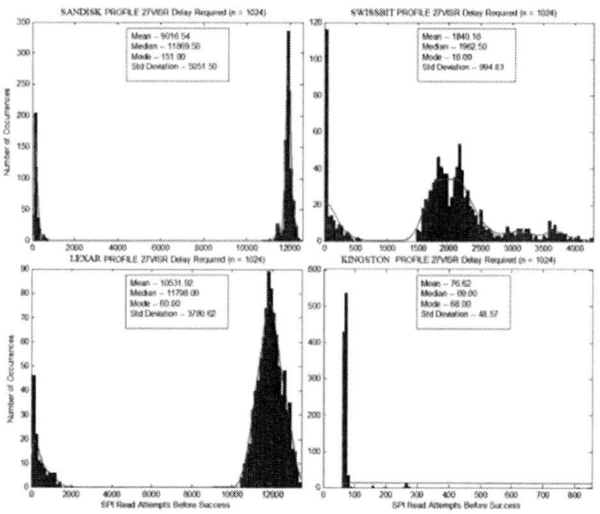

Figure 11: Timing Performance among Tested SD-Cards

TABLE IV. MICRO-SD CARD PACER RESULTS

Stage	Energy Results (uJ)				
	Control	***PACER-C***	***Diff.***	***PACER+IODVS***	***Diff.***
Sandisk	17066	15198	10.9%	11848	30.6%
Lexar	22707	21428	5.6%	16977	25.24
Swissbit	2763	914	66.9%	554	80.0%
Kingston	942	933	0.9%	897	4.8%

E. *Honeywell HIH-6130 Temperature / Humidity Sensor*

The Honeywell HIH-6130 communicates via the I^2C bus. The host requests the sensor to take a measurement and then waits the manufacturer-specified 45ms for the measurement to complete. Finally, the host retrieves the completed measurement. PACER-E demonstrated the best performance among the algorithms, perhaps because of the capacitive nature of the peripheral ADC. The effects are shown in Figure 12 and the numeric results are presented in TABLE V.

The PACER-T algorithm also produced impressive results with a wait latency of 31.66ms and wait energy of 254.14uJ. Compared with PACER-E, the result corresponds with a *slightly* increased latency and energy consumption of 0.5% and 4.3% respectively. For some applications, the simplicity of the PACER-T implementation may be preferable when compared to the best performing PACER-E algorithm.

TABLE V. HONEYWELL HIH-6130 PACER RESULTS

Stage	Latency Results (ms)				
	Control	***PACER-E***	***Diff.***	***PACER+IODVS***	***Diff.***
Wait	45.27	31.45	66.6%	19.27	66.6%
All	45.99	32.17	53.8%	32.95	53.8%
	Energy Results (uJ)				
Wait	325.95	240.29	26.3%	169.62	48.0%
All	330.50	245.39	25.8%	173.89	47.4%

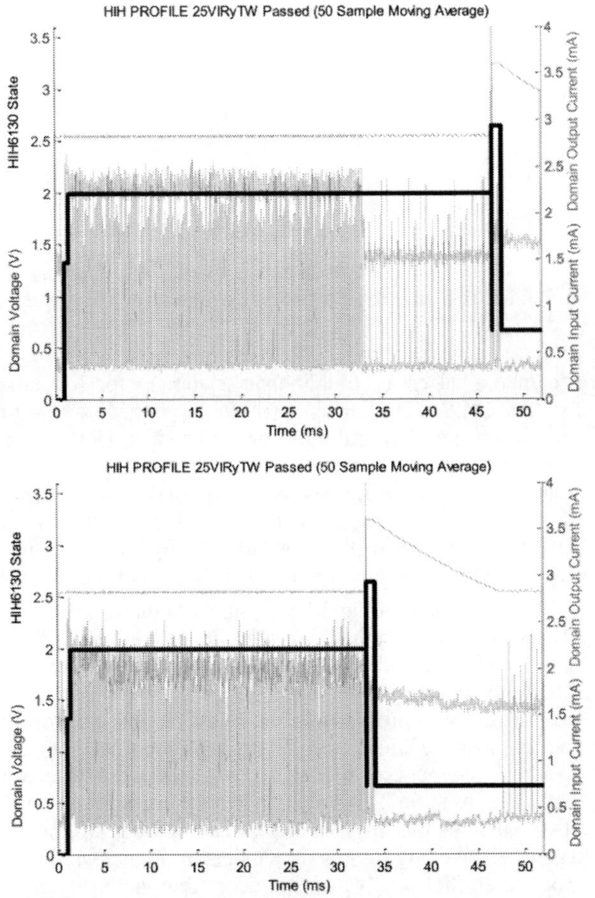

Figure 12: HIH-6130 Measurement Cycle Using IODVS and PACER-E

VI. CONCLUSIONS

Applying the PACER suite of algorithms to a variety of common embedded peripherals resulted in significant reductions to both latency and energy consumption. The PACER-T algorithm performed best against time-bound operations and was very competitive in energy-bound operations. For non-deterministic operations, the PACER-C algorithm performed well. When measured against a median baseline, the algorithm performed even better as the operational latency increased in randomness.

The PACER-T and PACER-E algorithms use successive approximation and the PACER-C algorithm uses a return-to-idle measurement to determine activity completion. It is likely that the performance of both methods could be enhanced further through the application of more complex algorithms. PACER-T could be applied to memory operations with a bimodal delay distribution by first testing for a cache hit and then delaying for a determined cache-miss time. Likewise, the PACER-C algorithm could be modified online so as to identify the current waveform features corresponding varying latencies, thus allowing the MCU to sleep longer.

As the cost of computation in embedded systems continues to decrease, it is natural to devote more computational resources to minimizing system-wide energy consumption and latency. The PACER suite of algorithms use minimal computational resources and are shown to decrease latency by up to 67% and device energy consumption by up to 80% when compared to the naïve worst-case estimate.

REFERENCES

[1] B. Brock and K. Rajamani, "Dynamic power management for embedded systems [SOC design]" IEEE International [Systems-on-Chip] SOC Conference 2003, Sept. 2003, pp. 416-419

[2] C. Kumar, M. Sindhwani, and T. Srikanthan, "Profile-based technique for Dynamic Power Management in embedded systems" International Conference on Electronic Design (ICED) 2008, Dec. 2008, pp. 1-6

[3] W. Dargie, "Dynamic Power Management in Wireless Sensor Networks: State-of-the-Art" IEEE Sensors Journal 2012, vol. 12, no. 5, pp. 1518-1528

[4] D. Moore and A. Dean, "Intra-Operation Dynamic Voltage Scaling" IEEE 3rd International Conference on Cyber-Physical Systems, Networks, and Applications, Aug. 2015, pp. 70-77

[5] D. Lee et al., "Adaptive-latency DRAM: Optimizing DRAM timing for the common-case" IEEE 21st International Symposium on High Performance Computer Architecture (HPCA), Feb. 2015, pp. 489-501

[6] S. Sadeghi-Kohan, M. Kamal, J. McNeil, P. Prinetto, and Z. Navabi, "Online self adjusting progressive age monitoring of timing variations" 10th International Conference on Design & Technology of Integrated Systems in Nanoscale Era (DTIS), Apr. 2015, pp. 1-2

[7] D. Etter, "Adaptive Estimation of Time Delays in Sampled Data Systems" IEEE Transactions on Acoustics Speech and Signal Processing, Jun. 1981, pp. 582-587

[8] V. Tarasov, G. Sim, A. Povzner, and E. Zadok, "Efficient I/O Scheduling with Accurately Estimated Disk Drive Latencies" The Proceedings of OSPERT 2012, July 2012, pp. 36-45

[9] H. Macicior et al., "Iterative capacity estimation of LiFePO4 cell over the lifecycle based on SoC estimation correction" Electric Vehicle Symposium and Exhibition (EVS27), Nov. 2013, pp. 1-10

[10] H. Mahanta, A. Azad, and A. Khan, "Power analysis attack: A vulnerability to smart card security" International Conference on Signal Processing And Communication Engineering Systems (SPACES), Jan. 2015, pp. 506-510

[11] M. Petrvalsky, M. Drutarovsky, and M. Varchola, "Differential power analysis attack on ARM based AES implementation without explicit synchronization" Radioelektronika 2014 24th International Conference, Apr. 2014, pp. 1-4

A SPECK Based 3G Authentication Algorithm for Download onto IoT Security Modules

Keith Mayes

Information Security Group
Royal Holloway, University of London
Egham, UK
keith.mayes@rhul.ac.uk

Steve Babbage

Vodafone Group R&D
Vodafone Group Services Ltd.
Newbury, UK
steve.babbage@vodafone.com

***Abstract*—3G/4G mobile standards benefit from an authentication algorithm called MILENAGE that supports mutual authentication, protection against replay attack and generates session keys to protect confidentiality and integrity. Its usefulness attracts interest beyond the original usage, such as in securing diverse wireless and wired bearers used in Machine-to-Machine and Internet of Things (IoT) systems. The long-term reliance on one algorithm is a risk, and recently an alternative algorithm, called TUAK, was standardised as a safe-guard, should the Advanced Encryption Standard (AES) core of MILENAGE ever be found vulnerable. Previous performance evaluation of TUAK on Subscriber Identity Modules (SIM), found that it needed to be implemented in low level native code to satisfy system timing requirements; indeed this is usually the case for MILENAGE. However, deployed security modules, anticipated for the Internet of Things (IoT), generally provide access at an application layer, abstracted from the underlying hardware. Application layer implementation of TUAK was shown to be too slow to comply with standardised requirements and so an alternative faster algorithm was sought that could be downloaded and run in a compliant manner from the application level. The National Institute of Standards and Technology (NIST) has standardised a lightweight block-cipher called SPECK, and this paper describes work to create a SPECK alternative to MILENAGE and compares its performance with earlier results from TUAK.**

Keywords-3GPP; GSM; Keccak; SPECK; TUAK.

I. INTRODUCTION

This text describes follow-on work from an earlier study which evaluated the performance of the TUAK algorithm on multiple smart card platforms [1][2]. In this latest work, we sought an alternative algorithm that had credible security, yet was fast enough to be executed at a smart card application layer (rather than native code) and meet standardised performance requirements. We will start by recapping on the MILENAGE and TUAK 3G algorithms.

The Third Generation Partnership Project (3GPP) [3] has standardised an algorithm framework that permits Mobile Network Operators (MNO) to select/design their own particular cryptographic algorithms for subscriber authentication and session key generation. However, in practice, most MNOs have adopted the MILENAGE algorithm [4] that is based on AES [5]. MILENAGE is an openly evaluated and peer-reviewed example algorithm, originally designed and published by the European Telecommunications Standards Institute (ETSI) [6], Security Algorithms Group of Experts (SAGE). The security of MILENAGE is well respected, which in part accounts for its widespread use; although the use of a common approach becomes a necessity (rather than a choice) for Machine-to-machine (M2M) applications, where the particular MNO may need to change during the life of the product. Ubiquitous use of a single algorithm in equipment that may be used for many years carries a security risk, and so SAGE has standardised an alternative algorithm, called TUAK [7], which has a very different structure to MILENAGE, being built around the Keccak [8] sponge function used in the SHA3 algorithm [9].

As well as running in a system Authentication Centre (AuC), the 3G authentication algorithms must be capable of running on Subscriber Identity Modules (SIM), which are essentially smart card platforms with very restricted resources, both in terms of processor speed and available memory. It is possible to have smart cards with crypto-coprocessors, which greatly accelerate common algorithms, however these are normally not used in SIMs due to cost constraints. Therefore, SIM platforms that may offer application layer programming, typically have algorithms implemented in native code, for speed and efficiency, which are accessible via an Application Programming Interface (API). Previous work has shown that the native code approach would allow a TUAK implementation to meet the standardised performance requirements, however, application layer implementation would not. This is fine in a traditional MNO Issuer model as the native code can be defined, but it is a problem if we have to host algorithms on pre-existing general purpose SIM modules, where we only have access at the application layer.

This latter situation is increasingly likely if we now consider a future where our M2M solutions are provided in the much wider and general-purpose context of the Internet of Things (IoT). The resulting research question, is whether we can find an alternative to MILENAGE and TUAK, which meets best-practice security, yet is fast enough to be implemented at a SIM application layer and still meet the standardised performance requirements.

In Section II, an overview of MILENAGE and TUAK is provided, before introducing the SPECK algorithm in Section III. Implementation of the SPECK cipher on MULTOS is discussed in Section IV, along with some initial results. Section V describes the use of SPECK within 3G authentication, and presents the experimental results. Conclusions and suggestions for future work are offered in Section VI.

II. MILENAGE AND TUAK

In this section, we will briefly consider MILENAGE and TUAK, before suggesting how SPECK might be introduced,

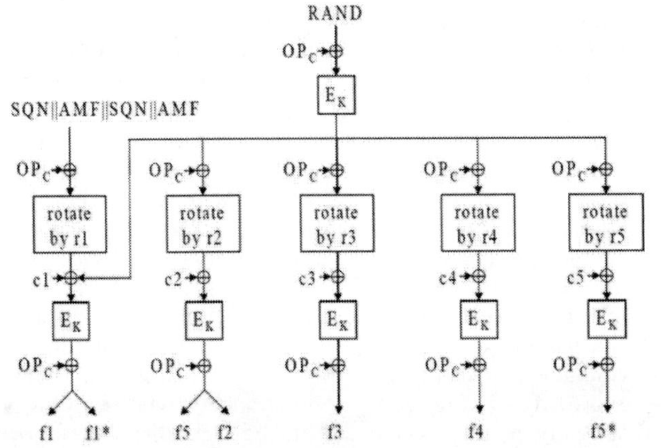

Figure 1. MILENAGE

to offer a third option for providing the mobile communication authentication and key agreement functions, specified by 3GPP for UMTS (3G) and the Long Term Evolution (LTE 4G) in [10].

A. MILENAGE

The 3G authentication solution follows a challenge-response approach similar to the earlier GSM solution, except that the challenge and responses are expanded for improved security. The structure of MILENAGE is shown in Figure 1. The challenge is 256 bits long and made up of a 128-bit random number (RAND), a 64-bit Message Authentication Code (MAC), a 48-bit sequence number (SQN) and a 16-bit management field (AMF). The MAC is recomputed on the SIM (f1 in the diagram), to ensure that the challenge was created by the genuine AuC, and the SQN is used to check that the challenge is fresh and not re-played. The result from the authentication (XRES), which is returned to the challenger, is 32-128 bits long. The algorithm generates two session keys for local storage/use, a 128-bit cipher key (CK) and a 128-bit integrity key (IK). The 48-bit anonymity key (AK) can be used during the authentication process to conceal the true value of SQN. AMF permits some home operator control of the authentication process, but is not relevant to this discussion. Within Figure 1, the repeated use of a block cipher (E_K) can be seen, which in MILENAGE is based on AES [5]. The OPc value is computed from an operator customisation value OP, however it is normal to store the pre-computed OPc within the SIM.

B. the TUAK Algorithm

The structure at the core of TUAK, as can be seen in Figure 2, is nothing like MILENAGE, as it is based on the Keccak [8] "cryptographic sponge function" [11]. This function has a good security pedigree as it is used in the SHA-3 hash function [9] and its security design properties have been investigated [12]. The authentication function is implemented by absorbing the challenge related data into the sponge, running the algorithm and then squeezing out the result and keys as shown in Figure 3. TOPc is analogous to OPc and also pre-computed and stored in the SIM; so Keccak only needs to be run twice during an authentication. TUAK uses Keccak with permutation size n = 1600, capacity c = 512 and rate r = 1088, so that only

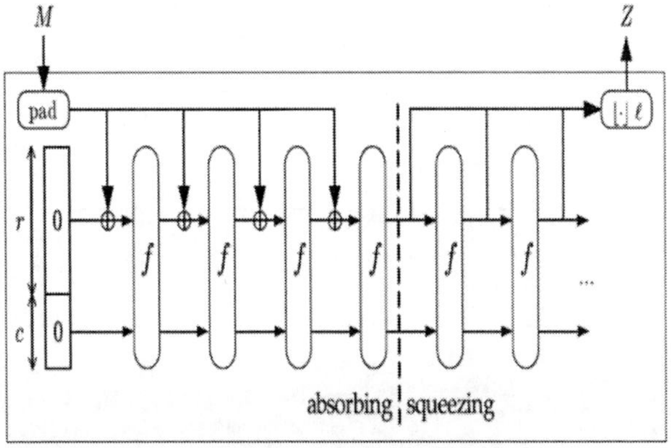

Figure 2. A Cryptographic Sponge Function

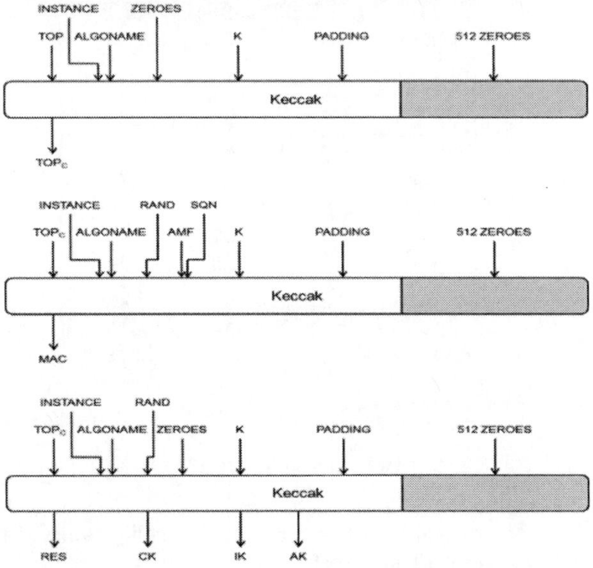

Figure 3. The TUAK Algorithm Functions

a single iteration of the permutation f is required at each stage. The feasibility of low-level native code implementation of TUAK on real secured smart card chips was first proven in [1], although this result did not extend to application level processing. To achieve the latter, requires a significantly faster core function. There are numerous candidates for such a function, however, the private research project on which this publication is based, was to specifically consider "SPECK" [13] as an alternative to the AES-based MILENAGE.

III. SPECK

SPECK is a family of block ciphers designed by a group of researchers from the NSA. SPECK, together with its sister cipher SIMON, was first published in 2013 [13], and some additional design notes were released more recently [14]. Both algorithms are designed with constrained devices in mind: SPECK is designed to have a very small footprint in software, while SIMON is designed for hardware. SPECK is a lightweight block cipher specification intended specifically for efficient implementation on resource limited chips and its performance has already been studied for use in IoT [15]. However, that performance evaluation assumed that the

TABLE I. SPECK VARIANTS

Block size 2n	Key size mn	Word size n	Key words m	Rot α	Rot β	Rounds T
32	64	16	4	7	2	22
48	72	24	3	8	3	22
	96		4			23
64	96	32	3	8	3	26
	128		4			27
96	96	48	2	8	3	28
	144		3			29
128	128	64	2	8	3	32
	192		3			33
	256		4			34

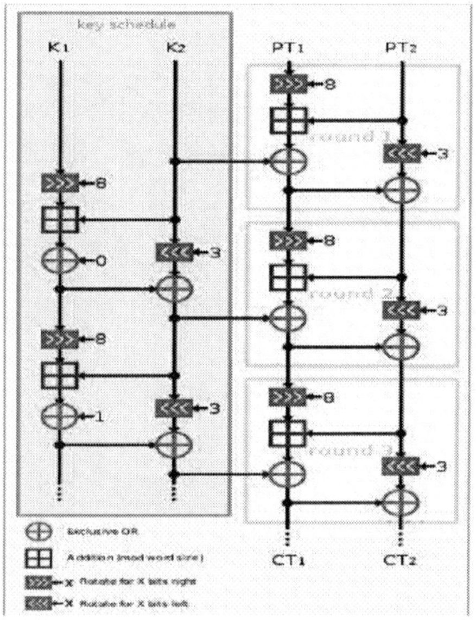

Figure 4. SPECK Overview [16]

algorithm would be native coded onto the chip, whereas here we are considering the post-issue loading of the algorithm onto a secure platform, which is abstracted from the underlying hardware and only accessible via controlled APIs.

SPECK is a family of multi-round ciphers with associated key schedules; the exact variant being defined by a number of design parameters as illustrated in Table I, which can be generally visualised in Figure 4 [16]. Note that this work found and reported an error in an earlier version of this reference diagram; which showed the K_1 XOR sequence, starting with '1' rather than '0'.

Referring back to Figure 1, the inputs and outputs to E_K are 128 bits and the minimum acceptable keysize is also 128 bits. Returning to Table I, we see that the 32 round SPECK (128/128) variant provides an ideal E_K candidate, with the 33 and 34 round being similar to the higher security modes offered in TUAK. The SPECK designers estimate that the (128/128) variant can be implemented in less than half the memory of 128-bit AES, with throughput some 70% higher. When implementing SPECK authentication, we used the same r and c parameters from the MILENAGE specification, and followed the common-practice of pre-computing OPc and storing in smart card memory

SIMON and SPECK have attracted a fair amount of attention from cryptographers, and several cryptanalysis papers have been published, attacking reduced round versions of the ciphers. Early differential cryptanalysis by Abed et al [17] and Dinur [18] performed better than simplistic exhaustive key search (albeit with a very large number of chosen plaintexts) for up to 17 rounds of SPECK; later work by Fu et al [19] extended this to 22 rounds, and then Song et al [20] to 23 rounds. Differential attacks on reduced-round versions of other members of the SPECK family have also been found by Biryukov et al [21]. Linear cryptanalysis has also been attempted, by Liu et al [22], but with less success than the differential attacks. There is thus a significant security margin between the number of rounds attacked (23) and the full number of rounds (32) in our selected variant, justifying confidence in the cipher. However, the NSA origins of SPECK and SIMON worry some cryptographers, who fear that NSA are only promoting the ciphers because they know how to break them. Notably, attempts to have SIMON and SPECK standardised by ISO have been repeatedly defeated [23]. It is not possible to determine if these suspicions have any basis in fact, so we will consider our proposal justified, based on the existing body of published security research work.

IV. Implementing the SPECK Cipher on MULTOS

Performance studies on smart cards and microcontrollers often make an assumption that an application has low-level direct access to the CPU. This is typically not the case in secure implementations, especially when the platform is intended to be strongly attack resistant. The access/interface is often via secured operating systems and virtual machines that intentionally abstract an application from the underlying hardware. MULTOS [24] cards/chips are good examples of secured platforms that work this way and results are available from the TUAK study. The SPECK MULTOS results will provide an interesting comparison to the native coded implementation in the later stage of the study. It is also worth noting that MULTOS has been proposed for use in IoT due to its capability for secure application loading/management (PKI based) in the field. The implementation approach for MULTOS is to initially develop the SPECK code on a simulator and then load onto a real card for performance measurement. We will start with a naive implementation based on published pseudo code to first check compliance with the associated test vectors. We will then refine/optimise the implementation as we progress through the study. We know from previous work that MULTOS performance struggles when a variable parameter is used to control the extent of block shifts/rotates, and so it is suspected that the naive implementation of SPECK will be slow, as it follows the pseudo code and specifies the shift amounts as variables. Once we have confidence in the core SPECK implementation we will fit it within the 3G authentication framework for the comparative (with TUAK) performance tests.

A. *Initial Results/Observations*

Considering the simplicity of the SPECK cipher there were some unexpected difficulties in creating a version which produced the correct test vector result. Firstly, the 'C' code examples for the 128/128 mode use 64-bit unsigned integers (uint64_t) that are not universally supported by 'C' compilers, especially for legacy and specialist secured microcontrollers. This meant that the pseudo code could not be used unmodified as the starting point. Of course as the target CPU is 16-bit, the

TABLE II. INITIAL MULTOS FUNCTIONAL TEST RESULTS

Test Type	Execution Time (ms)	Comment
Null	43	Command handling and 16 bytes of data in message response, with no actual function performed. This has already been subtracted from other results
SPECK	253	Full cipher 128/128 functionally correct and producing correct test vector result [No MULTOS primitives]
SPECK	157	Uses pre-computed key-schedule (256 bytes) [No MULTOS primitives]
Rotate Right 8 places	1.01	[No MULTOS primitives]
Rotate Left 3 places	1.84	[No MULTOS primitives]
Add 64 bit results	1.25	[No MULTOS primitives]

compiler would just have to mimic the manually coded creation of the 64-bit types. For convenience and efficiency, a union type was created so that the 64-bit storage could be accessed as constituent 32, 16 and 8 bit unsigned integers. In order to obtain intermediate round and key-schedule reference results it was decided to first implement the example code using the lcc compiler on a Windows PC and dump intermediate results to a log file, for later use in verifying the MULTOS implementation. Once the reference test version was working and the test results produced, the equivalent functionality was coded for the MULTOS platform. The initial style was reasonably efficient, avoiding unnecessary loops, function calls and stack-based parameter passing; and speed critical variables were created in reserved session RAM. The latter is important as non-volatile storage on the target microcontrollers is significantly slower than RAM. However, at this stage we did not use any MULTOS primitives so all the functionality was coded at the application layer. We did however provide an option to use a pre-computed key schedule as discussed below.

1) Key-schedule Pre-computation: In smart card devices it is quite normal to store a few kilobytes of sensitive account specific data (e.g., certificates, keys, photos, account details, IDs, PINs etc.) during the personalisation process. This data is stored in the non-volatile memory (characterised by fast reads and slower writes) that is shared with the code. For the SPECK cipher mode under consideration (128/128), we must at least store a 128bit (16 byte) long-term secret key 'K' . The key-schedule requires a 64 bit (8 byte) key for each round that is generated from 'K'. For a non-optimised solution the round function for round key generation is the same as for the data processing, so no significant extra code space would be required. An optimised version (avoiding parameter passing) would likely need some additional code space. Pre-computation of the key schedule would require 32x8 = 256 bytes of non-volatile memory which is by no means prohibitive, even in old smart cards. As Round is called almost as many times for round key generation as for the data processing, there is potential for significant speed improvement by using pre-computation.

Once the MULTOS code was functional it was loaded onto an ML3-80K-R1 MULTOS test card, which is based on the same Infineon SLE78 chip [25] that we used in the TUAK performance study. Commands were then sent to the card using the MULTOS scripting utility (MUTIL) and response times recorded. Table II, gives a summary of the first functional test results.

Often encoding an algorithm at the MULTOS application layer results in an implementation that is too slow to be practical; as was the case with TUAK. Although 253ms is not fast for running a block cipher, it is not necessarily unusable and there is still the potential for speed-up by exploiting suitable MULTOS primitives. Furthermore, pre-computation and personalisation of long-term round keys is quite practical and so the 157ms execution time is considered the benchmark performance at this stage. We will explore the use of primitives in the next stage of the study when we will see if SPECK could satisfy the SAGE/GSMA performance requirements on a MULTOS platform.

TABLE III. RESULTS WITH AND WITHOUT PRIMITIVES

Test Type	No Primitives Execution Time (ms)	Primitives Execution Time (ms)
Null	43	43
SPECK (precomputed key-schedule)	154.57	84.34
Rotate 64 bits Right by 8 places	1.01	0.63
Rotate 64 bits Left by 3 places	1.84	0.83
Add 64 bit inputs	1.25	0.54
XOR 64 bit inputs	0.56	0.53

V. IMPLEMENTING 3G SPECK AUTHENTICATION ON MULTOS

The results so far have shown better performance than had been anticipated on the MULTOS platform, however they did not make use of standard primitives offered by the platform. Use of such primitives is advisable for performance, but also for security reasons as their implementation is likely to have been defensively coded and evaluated against attack

A. 4.1 Conversion to MULTOS Primitives

The SLE78 is an innovative security controller intended for high security applications. Instead of relying mainly on shields and sensors it uses "Integrity Guard", which exploits dual CPUs working in tandem. The supported primitives of main interest included:

- multosBlockShiftRight()
- multosBlockShiftLeft()
- multosBlockAdd()
- multosBlockXor()

Note that MULTOS does not offer block rotates, however these are simple to implement using the shift primitives. Prior to converting the initial code to make use of primitives and adding support for 3G authentication processing, some test commands were created to practically determine performance impact. The set of results are presented in Table III, for the case of a pre-computed key-schedule. Note that all the primitive test utilities also made use of multosBlockCopy().

Considering Table III, with the exception of XOR, all the basic functions roughly doubled in speed when using platform primitives; notably SPECK execution time reduced from 154.57ms to 84.34ms. XOR is a very simple function at the application layer and so little improvement (0.56ms to 0.53ms) was anticipated. The notable effect is that using the available primitives nearly doubles the overall speed of the SPECK block cipher. This is an interesting result for the 3G authentication comparison, as following the 3G MILENAGE structure, requires the block cipher to be called multiple times.

TABLE IV. MILENAGE FUNCTION MAPPING

Function	Mapping
f1	MAC-A 64 bits
f1*	MAC-S (alternative used in re-synch)
f2	RES 64 bits
f3	CK 128 bits (ciphering key)
f4	IK 128 bits (integrity key)
f5	AK 48 bits (anonymity key)
f5*	Alternative AK used in re-synch

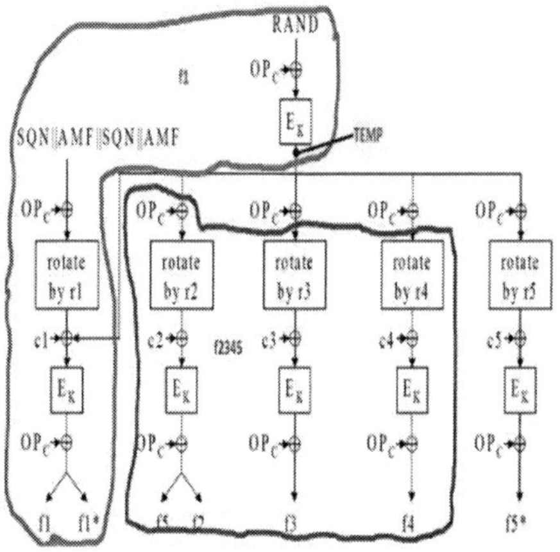

Figure 5. Implementation split of f1()and f2345()

B. Implementation of 3G Authentication

Referring back to Figure 3, we will adopt the same implementation approach as used for the earlier TUAK work so the results can be as closely comparable as possible. This requires development of two functions making use of the SPECK block cipher within the MILENAGE structure. The functions are separated in this way as they have different input values.

- SPECK_f1() computes f1 (and f1*)
- SPECK_f2345 computes f2, f3, f4, f5

The output of f5* is not part of a regular authentication vector (it is only used when resynchronisation of the sequence number SQN is needed), and so will not be included in our measurement. For clarity we present the mapping of these functions to the protocol, within Table IV.

We have reproduced the MILENAGE structure in Figure 5; showing the practical split of the f1 and f2345 functions.

When testing, it is assumed the f1() is run first so that the value TEMP can be re-used in f2345(), avoiding an extra encryption. Within f2345(), TEMP only needs to be XORed once with the (pre-computed) OPc. Considering the operations in addition to ciphering, we can see rotates and XORs using standardised values. Fortunately the rotates are easy when using the standard r values; r1 = 64, r2 = 0, r3 = 32, r4 = 64 (and r5 = 96). The integers are all multiples of 8 bits and so rotates can be performed simply with byte copies. The XORs with the c constants are also very simple as the values only affect the least significant byte, so byte, rather than block XORs are needed. The functions were coded using MULTOS primitives and the initial results are presented in Table V.

It can be seen from Table V, that the function times are dominated by the SPECK block cipher execution times. The total time (433.8ms) is very interesting as it fits within the

TABLE V. AUTHENTICATION FUNCTION EXECUTION TIMES (ms)

Function	Execution Time (ms)	Block Encryptions
f1()	173.16	2
f2345()	260.64	3
Total	433.80	5

TABLE VI. MULTOS TUAK AND SPECK AUTHENTICATION COMPARISON

Function	TUAK Authentication (ms)	SPECK Authentication (ms)
f1()	1529	173.16
f2345()	1575	260.64
Total	3104	433.80

revised performance specification proposed to SAGE during the TUAK study [26].

..."The functions f1-f5 and f1 shall be designed so that they can be implemented on a mid-range microprocessor IC card (typically 16-bit CPU), occupying no more than 8 kbytes non-volatile-memory (NVM), reserving no more than 300 bytes of RAM and producing AK, XMAC-A, RES, CK and IK in less than 500 ms total execution time."...*

Although the test implementation has no added high-level measures for defensive coding, the application is running on a MULTOS platform, which is marketed for its evaluated high-security capabilities. It would be expected that the platform's chip and native code would have defensive measures to counter fault and side-channel attacks. The fact that a platform level implementation can satisfy performance constraints suggests that the functionality could be added to stock or issued devices. This is a major operational advantage that was not available for the TUAK implementation. Although Java Card [27] is out of scope for this study, it is not unreasonable to consider that performance might also be adequate on that platform type; although it is possible that added defensive measures might be needed at the application layer.

C. MULTOS Comparison of SPECK with TUAK Authentication

A main purpose of this study was to see whether TUAK could be used as an alternative to SPECK in Internet of Things (IoT) type applications, where the processors have limitations similar to those of traditional smart cards. To measure this, the SPECK authentication functionality has been implemented in the same manner and on the same platforms as in the earlier TUAK study, so results are directly comparable. It may be recalled that TUAK did not suit MULTOS application implementation using existing primitives, as the comparison in Table VI shows. In fact, the TUAK authentication takes roughly 7x as long as SPECK.

MULTOS chips are being proposed for use in IoT applications and the results suggest that they could support SPECK on existing/standard platforms, whereas a custom primitive is essential for TUAK.

D. Native mode Comparison of SPECK with TUAK Authentication

Although this study was primarily focussed on downloading and running an authentication algorithm on a platform application layer, a native mode implementation was also created for the Samsung S3CCE9E4/8 chip (more detail in

TABLE VII. NATIVE MODE TUAK AND SPECK AUTHENTICATION COMPARISON

Function	TUAK Authentication (ms)	SPECK Authentication (ms)
f1()	77.88	3.35
f2345()	78.18	5.13
Total	156.06	8.48

[2]), which is a 16-bit secured smart card chip also used in the earlier TUAK performance study. For interest, the comparative results are presented in Table VII.

Clearly the native SPECK implementation is very fast (8.48ms) even on an old chip, but the result should be viewed with caution as there are no defensive coding measures in place, which could easily add an order of magnitude to the execution time.

VI. Conclusions and Future Work

The experiments conducted during this project have shown that the SPECK cipher is significantly faster than Keccak (TUAK core) when implemented on the MULTOS platform (or indeed in native mode). The results from the MILENAGE style authentication using SPECK, were significant as they showed that a MULTOS application layer implementation could satisfy the 3GPP timing constraints; something that was not possible with TUAK. There would even be headroom to add a few extra rounds to the SPECK function to increase its security margin, if preferred. This means that the algorithm could be loaded and configured post-issue, which has relevance for M2M and general IoT devices. In fact, MULTOS has begun to position itself in IoT because apart from its secure design, it also has an application loading mechanism based on PKI. This means devices can be configured offline, outside of secure environments, and without the need to distribute shared secret keys. 3GPP does not specify a standard algorithm, but rather a framework with MILENAGE and TUAK presented as example implementations; and so the SPECK version could be used within the standard. For the future, it would be interesting to implement the SPECK-based 3G authentication on a Java Card and compare the results with the MULTOS platform results.

Acknowledgment

The authors would like to thank the UK National Cyber Security Centre (NCSC) for its support of this work.

References

[1] K. Mayes, S. Babbage, and A. Maximov, "Performance Evaluation of the new TUAK Mobile Authentication Algorithm", in Proc. ICONS/EMBEDDED, pp. 38-44, 2016.

[2] K. Mayes and S, Babbage, "A Multi-Platform Performance Evaluation of the TUAK Mobile Authentication Algorithm", International Journal on Advances in Security, vol 9, no. 3&4, pp. 158-168, 2016.

[3] (2017, Oct.) The Third Generation Partnership Project website, [Online]. Available: http://www.3gpp.org/, [retrieved: March, 2018].

[4] 3GPP TS 35.206: 3G Security; Specification of the MILENAGE algorithm set: An example algorithm set for the 3GPP authentication and key generation functions f1, f1*, f2, f3, f4, f5 and f5*; Document 2: Algorithm specification (2014).

[5] Federal Information processing Standards, Advanced Encryption Standard (AES), FIPS publication 197 (2001).

[6] (2017, Oct.) The European Telecommunications Standards Institute website, [Online]. Available: http://www.etsi.org/, [retrieved: March, 2018].

[7] 3GPP, TS 35.231: 3G Security; Specification of the TUAK algorithm set: A second example algorithm set for the 3GPP authentication and key generation functions f1, f1*, f2, f3, f4, f5 and f5*; Document 1: Algorithm specification (2014).

[8] G. Bertoni, J. Daemen, M. Peeters, and G. van Aasche, "The keccak Reference", version 3.0, 14 (2011).

[9] NIST, Announcing Draft Federal Information Processing Standard (FIPS) 202, SHA-3 Standard: Permutation-Based Hash and Extendable-Output Functions, and Draft Revision of the Applicability Clause of FIPS 180-4, Secure Hash Standard, and Request for Comments, (2004).

[10] 3GPP, TS 33.102: UMTS 3G Security; Security Architecture, V11.5.1 (2013).

[11] G. Bertoni, J. Daemen, M. Peeters, and G. van Aasche, "Cryptographic Sponge Functions", version 0.1, (2011).

[12] G. Gong, K. Mandal, Y. Tan, and T.Wu, "Security Assessment of TUAK Algorithm Set", [Online]. Available: http://www.3gpp.org/ftp/Specs/archive/35_series/35.935/SAGE_report/Secassesment.zip (2014), [retrieved: March, 2018].

[13] R. Beaulieu, et al, The SIMON and SPECK Families of Lightweight Block Ciphers, Cryptology ePrint Archive, Report 2013/404, 2013, [Online]. Available: http://eprint.iacr.org/2013/404, [retrieved: March, 2018].

[14] R. Beaulieu, et al, Notes on the design and analysis of SIMON and SPECK, Cryptology ePrint Archive: Report 2017/560, 2017, [Online]. Available: http://eprint.iacr.org/2017/560, [retrieved: March, 2018].

[15] R. Beaulieu, et al, Simon and Speck: Block Ciphers for the Internet of Things, National Security Agency, (2015).

[16] (2017 Oct.) Wikipedia, Speck (cipher), [Online]. Available: https://en.wikipedia.org/wiki/Speck_(cipher), [retrieved: March, 2018].

[17] F. Abed, E. List, S. Lucks, and J. Wenzel, Cryptanalysis of the speck family of block ciphers, Cryptology ePrint Archive, Report 2013/568, 2013, [Online]. Available: http://eprint.iacr.org/2013/568, [retrieved: March, 2018].

[18] I.Dinur, Improved Differential Cryptanalysis of Round-Reduced Speck, Cryptology ePrint Archive: Report 2014/320, [Online]. Available: http://eprint.iacr.org/2014/320, [retrieved: March, 2018].

[19] K.Fu; et al, MILP-Based Automatic Search Algorithms for Differential and Linear Trails for Speck, Cryptology ePrint Archive: Report 2016/407, [Online]. Available: http://eprint.iacr.org/2016/407, [retrieved: March, 2018].

[20] L.Song, Z.Huang, and Q.Yang, Automatic Differential Analysis of ARX Block Ciphers with Application to SPECK and LEA, Cryptology ePrint Archive: Report 2016/209, [Online]. Available: http://eprint.iacr.org/2016/209, [retrieved: March, 2018].

[21] A.Biryukov, A.Roy, and V.Velichkov, Differential Analysis of Block Ciphers SIMON and SPECK, Cryptology ePrint Archive: Report 2014/922, [Online]. Available: http://eprint.iacr.org/2014/922, [retrieved: March, 2018].

[22] Y.Liu, et al, Linear cryptanalysis of reducedround SPECK, Information Processing Letters Volume 116, Issue 3, March 2016.

[23] CNBC News, Distrustful US allies force spy agency to back down in encryption row, September 2017, [Online]. Available: https://www.cnbc.com/2017/09/21/distrustfulusalliesforcensatoback-downinencryptionrow.html, [retrieved: March, 2018].

[24] (2017, Oct.) MULTOS website, [Online]. Available: http://www.multos.com/, [retrieved: March, 2018].

[25] (2017, Oct.) Infineon, SLE 78 family of 16-bit security controllers, [Online]. Available: https://www.infineon.com/cms/en/product/security-and-smart-card-solutions/security-controllers/sle78/channel.html?channel=5546d462503812bb015066c2d8e91745, [retrieved: March, 2018].

[26] (2017, Oct.) K. Mayes, "Performance Evaluation of the TUAK algorithm in support of the ETSI Sage standardisation group", 3GPP, 2014, [Online]. Available: at http://www.3gpp.org/ftp/Specs/archive/35_series/35.936/SAGE_report/Perfevaluation.zip, [retrieved: March, 2018].

[27] Oracle, Java Card Platform Specifications V3.04, (2011).

Thermoacoustics Analysis in a Rijke Tube

Israel Mejia Alonso
Eloy Edmundo Rodríguez Vázquez
Carlos Alexander Núñez Martín
Celso Eduardo Cruz González
National Research Laboratory on Cooling Technology (LaNITeF)
CIDESI
Querétaro, México
email: {imejia, erodriguez}@cidesi.edu.mx
cnunez@posgrado.cidesi.edu.mx

Celso Eduardo Cruz González
Engineering Center for Industrial Development (CIDESI)
Advanced Manufacturing Department
Cd. de México, México
email: ecruz@cidesi.edu.mx

Abstract—**This paper deals with the perturbation induced by the gauge pressure alongside a combustion chamber. This perturbation is modeled by acoustic pressure, measured at the end of the combustor. These vibration modes are obtained experimentally using Fourier Analysis. The analytic model of Pressure Distribution Equation (PDE) on can combustor is based on a wave equation. This paper describes the procedure that was carried out to obtain the temperature of a column of hot air inside a simple combustor. The Rijke tube was used with the aim of laying the foundations of a future thermoacoustic phenomenon analysis. The contribution of this work is spatial interpretation of pressure waves and displacement in a chamber during thermoacoustic phenomena.**

Keywords- Acoustics; Rijke tube; Thermodynamics, FFT analisys.

I. INTRODUCTION

The main indicator for acoustics phenomena is the excessive heat released that generates pressure oscillations in the combustion chamber. That relationship between heat and sound was discovered by Rayleigh [1] and formulated by Merkli [2]. Thermoacoustic instabilities can cause several problems in the fuel system such as efficiency degradation, premature wear of its components and even its catastrophic failure [3]. This phenomenon, in combination with high pressures and temperatures (including the incorrect fuel-air mixing process), produces highly polluting particles, such as NOx [4].

Nowadays, the state of the art related to thermoacoustic phenomena affecting gas turbines performance, has been mainly focused on some techniques as well as swirling flows [5] and [6]. Swirling flows provide aerodynamic stability to the combustion process by producing regions of recirculating flows that reduce the flame length and increase the residence time of the reactants in the flame zone [6]. Experimental analysis from combustion test rig using different kinds of injectors, constrictors, air-fuel mixes have been performed to find the best technique for combustion system [7]. Also, another analysis included premixed fluid and Helmholtz resonator [8].

The gas turbine combustion modelling and simulations and the acoustic phenomenon implies the necessity of implementing a control algorithm. The basic gas turbine model equations [9] are important for analysis, design and simulation of a control system especially for Combined Cycle Power Plants (CCPP) [10] and [11]. Focusing on acoustics, new passive and active control techniques for such instabilities have been studied and developed [12] as well as techniques of Adaptive Sliding Phasor Averaged Control (ASPAC: adapted the phase of the valve-commanded fuel flow variations) [13] and Multiscale extended Kalman (MSEK: predict the time-delayed states). These are promising techniques to reduce the energy consumption produced by pressure oscillations [14], but more research is required in this field.

The acoustic model proposed in this work has been planned to be the first part of a control algorithm to diminish the effect of the thermoacoustic phenomena into the can-combustor chamber. This research is carried out in CIDESI Queretaro, for the National Laboratory for Cooling Technologies Research (LaNITeF).

The rest of the paper is structured as follows. Section II presents the analytical model of pressure oscillation trough air columns. Section III presents a Rijke tube experiment. Fourier analysis is required to find the fundamental mode. Speed of sound and properties of the medium, such as density, are required to determine the parameter values of PDE. Section IV describes the results and validation of the model. Conclusions are presented in Section V. Section VI is related to future work.

II. ANALYTICAL MODEL OF PRESSURE OSCILLATION

Direct transformation between thermal energy and acoustic energy is called thermoacoustic phenomenon. Three conditions are required for this transformation to occur: (1) the medium must be a compressible fluid; (2) a temperature gradient must exist, and (3) the control volume must be contained by a physical border (chamber).

The wave equation is a linear second-order partial differential equation which describes the propagation of oscillations. The goal of this section is to establish a wave equation formulation in air column when thermoacoustic phenomena appear.

A. Stationary wave in air column

The wave equation for acoustic pressure is given by [15]

$$\frac{\partial^2 \xi}{\partial t^2} = \frac{\kappa}{\rho_0} \frac{\partial^2 \xi}{\partial x^2} \quad (1)$$

where, ξ is the displacement in the air, κ is bulk modulus for the air and ρ_0 is the density of the air under equilibrium conditions. The wave equation solution for acoustic pressure can be solved via separation of variables. A standing wave is created by superposition of two waves which travel in opposite directions in the medium with the same amplitude, see equation (2).

$$\xi(x,t) = 2\xi_0 \sin(kx)\cos(\omega t) \quad (2)$$

Index k corresponds to a wavenumber, ξ_0 is the signal amplitude and ω is the angular frequency. The Taylor'law for fluid [15] is used to formulate a standing waves pressure on air column.

$$p - p_o = \kappa \frac{\partial \xi}{\partial x} \quad (3)$$

$$P(x,t) = -2\xi_0 \kappa k \cos(kx)\cos(\omega t) \quad (4)$$

Equation (4) describes the distribution of pressures with no boundary conditions. The boundary conditions are given by the pressure nodes appearing inside an open tube on both sides.

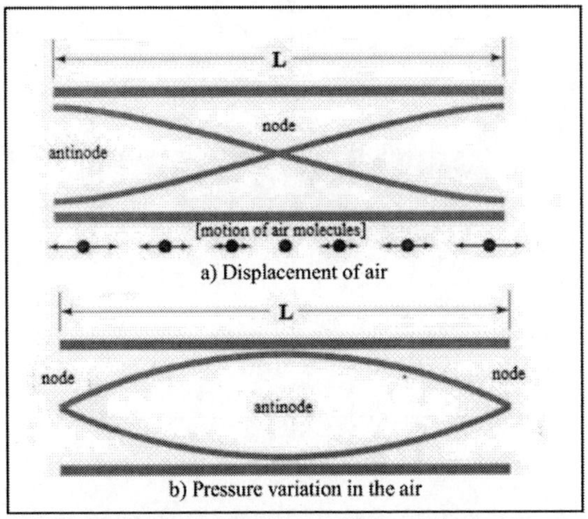

Figure 1. Pressure and displacement for the air in the columns.

B. Pipe open at both ends

A tube open at both ends provides a physical border from air column. At the open ends, the reflection that occurs is a function of the extension of the tube and the opening, compared to the wavelength that propagates through the tube. The inside of the tube is too narrow, and it is not possible to dissipate all the energy in the open end. This is because the phenomenon of reflection takes place. The reflection causes nodes and antinodes of pressure and displacement, see Figure 1.

Displacement nodes are associated with motion of air molecules, or modal modes. Otherwise, each end of the column must be a pressure node because the atmosphere cannot allow significant pressure change [16]. Also, (3) shows the relationship between pressure and motion of the air.

The general one-dimensional equation that describes the pressure distribution of a gas contained in a cylindrical combustor is obtained considering boundary conditions:

1. $P(0,t) = 0$
2. $P(L,t) = 0$

Form (4), the PDE model has been formulated as:

$$P(x,t) = -2\kappa k \xi \cos(k(x + \pi/2k))\cos(\omega t) \quad (5)$$

From the boundary conditions evaluation, the obtained PDE coefficients are:

Condition 1:

$$\begin{aligned} P((0),t) &= -2\kappa k \xi \cos(k((0) + \pi/2k))\cos(\omega t) \\ 0 &= \cos(\pi/2)\cos(\omega t) \\ 0 &= 0 \end{aligned}$$

Condition 2:

$$\begin{aligned} P((L),t) &= -2\kappa k \xi \cos(k((\pi/k) + \pi/2k))\cos(\omega t) \\ 0 &= \cos(3\pi/2)\cos(\omega t) \\ 0 &= 0 \end{aligned}$$

The one-dimension PDE on can combustor is shown in (6).

$$P(x,t) = -2kc^2 \rho \xi \cos(k((\pi/k) + \pi/2k))\cos(\omega t) \quad (6)$$

III. RIJKE TUBE EXPERIMENT

Thermoacoustics is concerned on the interactions between heat (thermos) and pressure oscillations in gases (acoustics). A "Rijke Tube", named after its inventor, is a fundamental tool for studying the thermoacoustic phenomenon. Rijke's tube turns heat into sound by creating a self-amplifying standing wave. This open cylinder resonator contains a metallic copper mesh positioned about one-fifth of the way up the tube. When the screen is heated in a burner flame and then moved to one side of the flame, it will produce a strong tone at its resonant frequency for several seconds.

An experiment was carried out using the Rijke tube [11] which shows the presence of a thermoacoustic phenomenon, as depicted in Figure 2. A steel pipe of 0.6 m long and a diameter of 0.04445 m (1 ¾ in) and thickness 0.00121 m (18 gauge) was used, as illustrated in Figure 1. x_m is the distance (0.12m) where a metallic mesh was placed.

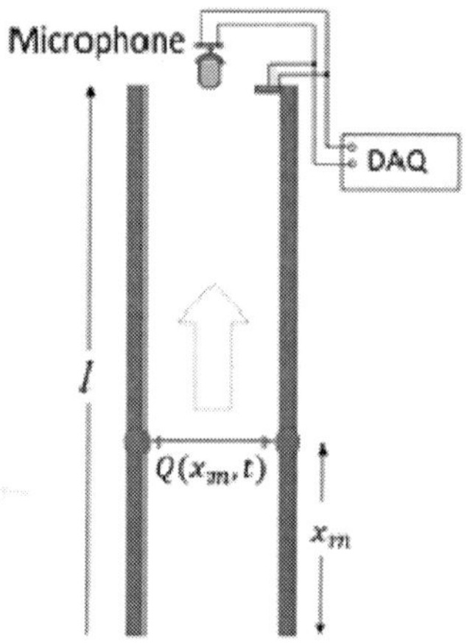

Figure 2. Data adquisition for Rijke tube experiment.

Rijke tube turns heat into sound by creating a self-amplifying standing wave. The heat source was provided by a gas thorn. The gas thorn adds energy to the system until the metallic mesh temperature rises to 600 °C. Then, the heat source is removed and the thermoacoustic phenomenon appears. It happens when the position of the pipe is vertical.

A. Fourier analysis

Time domain is the analysis physical signals of information with respect to time. It is beneficial when observing data such as temperature. However, some applications require analyzing the frequency components of signals, such as pressure oscillation of the air.

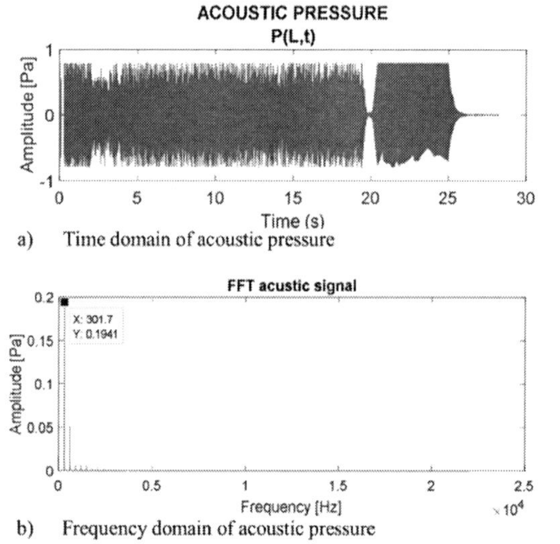

Figure 3.Signal analysis of acoustic pressure.

The acoustic pressure was measured using a microphone during the Rijke tube experiment. The same performance as in [17] was present. Time domain acoustic signal does not allow to see much information for analysis. A Fourier analysis was required. A Fast Fourier Transform (FFT) is an algorithm that samples a signal over a time (or space) period and divides it into its frequency components. FFT helps to find the fundamental frequency of the produced air column resonance.

The sampling frequency for the thermoacoustic test was 44100 samples per second. Fast Fourier Transform was applied with a resolution of 15 bits. Frequency resolution was about 1.34 Hz, which means that every 743 ms the algorithm takes a package sample to analyze.

Time-Frequency Signal Analysis Acoustic pressure was measured using a microphone. The signal for amplitude vs time is shown in Figure 3. The first modal mode occurs at 301 Hz with an amplitude of 0.1941 Pa.

B. Speed of sound of the air

The speed of sound is only affected by changes in the medium (density, humidity, temperature, etc.). For our case study, the element that changed significantly was the temperature.

On the other hand, the geometry of the combustor determines related terms like frequency and wavelength. The symbol λ is the length of the wave, that is, the space that the wave travels in a cycle. Figure 4 illustrates a reflection wave on pipe open ends. As both the output wave (green) and the reflected wave (red) only perform half a cycle inside the tube, the tube length is half the wavelength.

Consider just the motion of perturbation without the properties of the medium. The fundamental frequency is inversely proportional to the length of the tube.

$$c = \lambda f \tag{7}$$

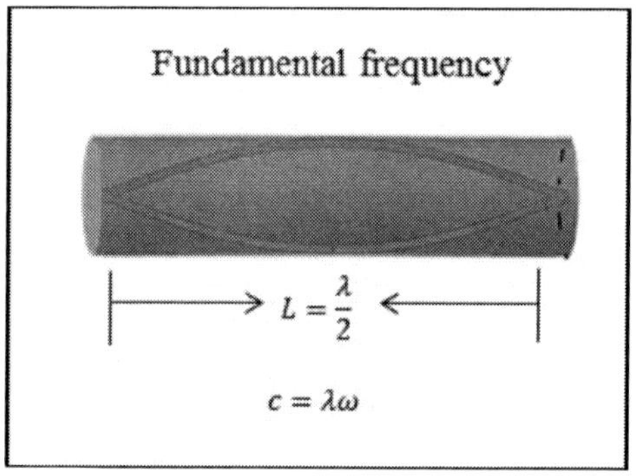

Figure 4. First vibration mode in air column.

In an ideal tube, the wavelength of the sound produced is directly proportional to the length of the tube. A tube which is open at one end and closed at the other produces sound with a wavelength equal to four times the length of the tube. In acoustics, end correction is a short distance applied or added to the actual length of a resonance pipe, to calculate the precise resonance frequency of the pipe. The pitch of a real tube is lower than the pitch predicted by the simple theory.

Equation (3) describe the end correction for pipe given in (8).

$$\lambda = 2(L + 0.61D) \tag{8}$$

The speed of sound result was 379.18 m/s.

C. *Temperature of the air*

Temperature is a physical quantity produced by motion of the molecules, which gives a perception of hot and cold. Temperature is associated with friction. Molecular friction is associated with pressure and density in the air. The ideal gas law is a good approximation of the behavior of many gases under many conditions, although it has several limitations.

The most frequently form of a state equation is given in (9).

$$\frac{P}{\rho} = \frac{RT}{M} \tag{9}$$

The acoustic wave velocity, c, depends on the material properties. Speed of sound is proportional to bulk modulus and inversely proportional to density of the air as dictated in (1).

$$\frac{\kappa}{\rho} = c^2$$

where $\kappa = \gamma P$ and γ is the heat capacity ratio. There is a strong relationship between pressure of the air, density of the air, temperature of the air and speed of sound [18] shown in (10).

$$\frac{\gamma P}{\rho} = c^2 = \frac{\gamma RT}{M} \tag{10}$$

Equation (10) infers that temperature can be expressed in terms of speed of sound.

$$T_{air} = \left(\frac{c_{air}}{20.055 \frac{m}{s \cdot K^{1/2}}} \right)^2 \tag{11}$$

Equation (11) was defined using nominal values of air.

The density of a substance is its mass per unit volume. The density can be changed by changing either the pressure or the temperature. Increasing the temperature generally decreases the density.

There are table properties of the air which have the density of the air in terms of temperature.

TABLE I. TEMPERATURE AND DENSITY OF THE AIR

Velocidad del sonido (m/s)	**T (°K)**	**T(°C)**	**ρ [Kg/m^3]**
379.18	357.48	84.48	0.9870

Table 1 shows the density of the air due to gradient of temperature. PDE variables are found.

IV. RESULTS

The one-dimension PDE on can combustor was formulated. The determination of parameter values was described in this paper.

$$P(x,t) = -2kc^2 \rho \xi \cos(k((\pi/k) + \pi/2k)) \cos(\omega t)$$

Pressure distribution along the can combustor is shown in Figure 5. This paper becomes useful for several combustor chambers with similar geometries.

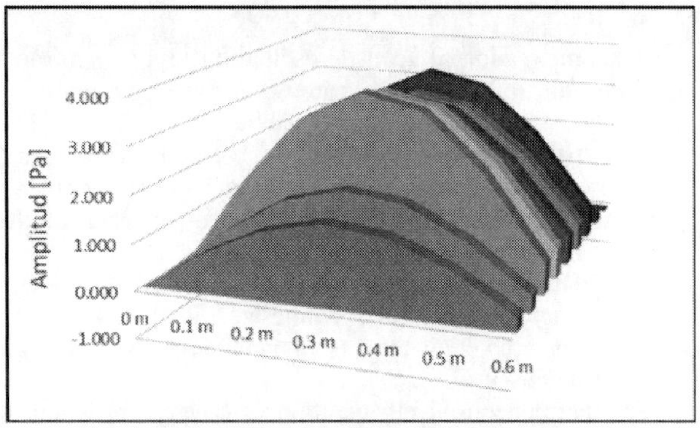

Figure 5. Fundamental mode of vibration in air column.

The result of the gradient of air temperature, within a finite volume and under conditions of natural convection, was the manifestation of the thermoacoustic phenomenon. The phenomena presence was used to validate the PDE model for the pressure oscillation inside the Rijke tube.

Advanced FFT Spectrum Analyzer was used to verify in real-time how the signal has grown. This is depicted in Figure 6.

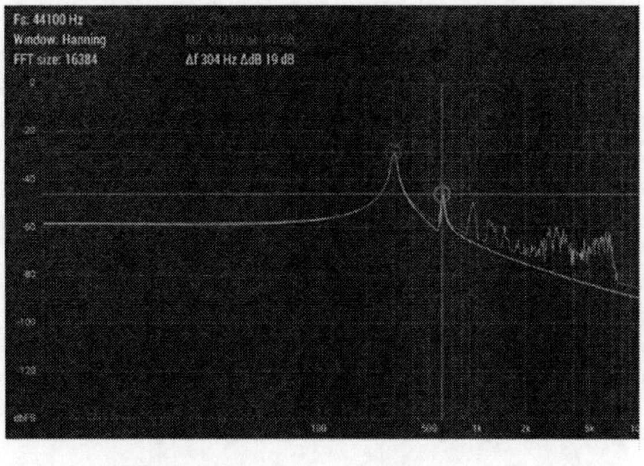

Figure 6. Fundamental frecuency measure on Rijke tube experiment.

It is demonstrated with the gas, due to its expansion and compression ratio, it will generate high pressure areas whose quality is directly proportional to the temperature of the medium. The melting temperature of the metal gauze oscillates around 600 °C at t=0 so convectively transferred the thermal energy and change the properties of the medium. The homologated temperature of the column was 78 ° C.

It was found experimentally that the speed of sound has been affected by the temperature change in the medium that propagates the disturbance, which was 379 m / s. Following the relationship in (1), we have the fundamental frequency of the gaseous fluid contained in a cylindrical geometry.

V. CONCLUSION

The propagation of acoustic oscillation in a compressive medium (air in this case), can be induced by applying thermal energy to the chambers' surface. The thermodynamic relationship between pressure, density and temperature has been verified for a single geometry combustor chamber, as well for this study in case of the Rijke tube.

The PDE model for the dynamic behavior of the pressure oscillation into a Rijke tube synthesized in this work was validated by predicting the first mode frequency of the air column pressure inside.

For thermoacoustic refrigeration, it is very important to know fluid dynamics and thermal behavior due to pressure oscillation.

VI. FUTURE WORK

The PDE model synthetized for the pressure distribution dynamics inside the chamber complemented in (11) to know the temperature behavior in the same volume, will be the basis of a control algorithm to regulate the thermal energy in the chamber surface to avoid or mitigate the effect of thermoacoustics.

ACKNOWLEDGMENT

The authors thank the Mexican Council for Science and Technology (CONACYT) for the support of both student's scholarships (437556 and 555423) and the LaNITeF Consolidation Project as well. The authors also thank the Advanced Manufacturing Department of CIDESI campus Edo. Mex. for the technology availability and collaboration.

REFERENCES

[1] J.W.S. B. Rayleigh, "The theory of sound" Book, Volume 2, London: Macmillan and Co. Cambridge 1877.

[2] P. Merkli and H Thomann, "Termoacoustic effects in a resonance tube", Journal of Fluid Mechanics, Volume 70, Cambridge University. July 1975.

[3] T. C. Lieuwen and V. Yang, "Combustion Instabilities in Gas Turbine Engines: Operational Experience, Fundamental Mechanisms and Modeling", American Institute of Aeronautics and Astronautics, 2006.

[4] M. O. Vigueras-Zuñiga, A. Valera-Medina, N. Syred, and P. Bowen, "High Momentum Flow Region and Central Recirculation Zone Interaction in Swirling Flows". Sociedad Mexicana de ingeriera Mecanica. vol. Vol. 4, pp. 195-204, 2014.

[5] S. Hochgreb, D. Dennis, and I. Ayranci, "Forced and Self-Excited Instabilities From Lean Premixed, Liquid-Fuelled Aeroengine Injectors at High Pressures and Temperatures" Turbine Technical Conference and Exposition, ASME Turbo Expo 2014.

[6] N. Yadav and A. Kushari. "Effect of swirl on the turbulent behaviour of a dump combustor flow", Journal of Aerospace Engineering, vol. 224, no. 6, pp. 705-717, 2010.

[7] A. Valera, A. Griffiths, and N. Syred, "Analysis of the Impact Caused by Coherent Structures in Swirling Flow Combustion Systems", Ingeniería investigación y Tecnologia, FI-UNAM, 2012.

[8] Z. Zhang, D. Zhao, N. Han, S. Wang, J. Li, "Control of combustion instability with a tunable Helmholtz resonator", Aerospace Science and Technology, Elsevier, 2014.

[9] W. Rowen. "Simplified mathematical representations of heavy-duty gas turbines", ASME J. Eng. Power, vol. 105, pp. 865-869, 2013.

[10] J. Rai, N. Hasan, B. Arora, R. Garai, R. Kapoor and Ibraheem. "Performance Analysis of CCGT Power Plant using MATLAB/Simulink Based Simulation", International Journal of Advancements in Research & Technology, vol. Volume 2, no. Issue 5, 2013.

[11] T. Samad and A. Annaswamy. "The impact of Control Technology", [Online] Available: ww.ieeecss.org, 2011

[12] A. Banaszuk, "Control of Combustion Inestability: From Passive to Active Control of Combustors", Grand Challenges for Control, IEEE, 2012.

[13] C. Dong, K. Jay, and J. Yong. "Analysis of the combustion instability of a model gas turbine combustor by the transfer matrix method", Journal of Mechanical Science and Technology, vol. 23, April, pp. 1602-1612, 2009.

[14] S. Kai-Uwe, K. Rainer and B. Hans-Jörg. "Experimental Characterization of Premixed Flame Instabilities of a Model Gas Turbine Burner". Flow, Turbulence and Combustion, vol. 76, no. 2, pp. 177-197, 2006.

[15] M. Alonso and E. Finn, "Physical: Waves and Fields" Book, Vol. II. Fondo Educativo Interamericano. Pp 694- 712

[16] Universidad de Valladolid, "Waves and propagation", Curso online:https://www.lpi.tel.uva.es/~nacho/docencia/ing_ond_1/trabajos_05_06/io2/public_html/viento/principios_viento.html. Abril 2017.

[17] S. Shariati, A. Franca, B. Oezer, R. Noske, D. Abel, A. Brockhinke, "Modeling and Model Predictive Control of Combustion Instabilities in a Multi-section Combustion Chamber Using Two-Port Elements", IEEE Multi-conference on Systems and Control, Antibes, France. 2014

[18] Y. Cengel and M. Boles, "Termodinamica" Book, 7th Edition, Mc Graw Hill, 2012.

[19] J. Mathews and F. Kurtis. "Numerical Methods Using Matlab". Fourth Edition. Prentice Hall New Jersey. Chapter 2, 2004.

[20] E. Gutiérrez, G. Vélez, D. Szwedowicz, J. Bedolla, C. Cortés. "Identification of Close Vibration Modes of a Quasi-Axisymmetric Structure: Complemetary Study". Ingeniería Investigación y Tenología.Vol XIV, Apr, pp. 207-222, 2012.

Dynamic Behavior Model for Cooling System Based on Vapor Compression

Experimental Analysis and Simulation Validation Grounded on a Reduced Order Differential Equation with Few Degrees of Freedom

Guillermo Domínguez Librado
National Research Laboratory on Cooling Technology
Engineering Center for Industrial Development (CIDESI)
Querétaro, México
e-mail: gdominguez@posgrado.cidesi.edu.mx

Eloy Edmundo Rodríguez Vázquez
National Research Laboratory on Cooling Technology
Engineering Center for Industrial Development (CIDESI)
Querétaro, México
e-mail: eloy.rodriguez@cidesi.edu.mx

Luis Alvaro Montoya Santiyanes
National Research Laboratory on Cooling Technology
Engineering Center for Industrial Development (CIDESI)
Querétaro, México
e-mail: lmontoya@posgrado.cidesi.edu.mx

Hugo Gamez Cuatzin
CIDESI campus Estado de Mexico
Estado de México
hgamez@cidesi.edu.mx

***Abstract*—This article presents the dynamic analysis of a single-stage vapor-compression refrigeration system. The model is based on the development of submodels for each component of the refrigeration system, applying the space state approach. The developing and verification of dynamic models for different configurations of thermal systems is critical in order to design control algorithms with optimal energy consumption. This analysis culminates with the comparison between direct performance of the refrigerant R134a as working fluid and the behavior temperature of the compartment in a refrigerator and the results obtained are similar in the evaporator temperature and pressure.**

Keywords-Heat exchangers; Refrigerants; Dynamic Model; Household refrigeration.

I. Introduction

Refrigeration and air conditioning is an active, rapidly developing technology. It is closely related to the living standard of the people and to the outdoor environment, such as through ozone depletion and global warming.

Mathematical modeling is the most practical way of studying the basic behavior of cycle performance, the relative losses in various components and interactions of their performance characteristics. Standard science and engineering formulations are applied to describe mathematically the basics processes occurring in the Vapor Compressor Refrigerating (VCR) systems. Mathematical modeling is not an end in itself but is a step towards simulation optimization.

The dynamic modeling of VCR system has been subject on interest since the late 1970s, where first principle models were used to describe the heat exchangers. Lumped parameters, moving boundary models [1]-[3], and then McArthur initiated a series of works focus on a distributed parameters formulation [4]. Besides this main modeling stream, other authors have designed more complex model for analyzing specific phenomena but we refer to review of [5] and to subsequent works and the references therein [6][7]. Later on in 1990s traditional feedback control has also been investigated, as in [8] and, more recently, multivariable control strategy have been developed, [6][7][9][10]; in other studies, Jensen and Skogestad 2007a, b [11][12], strategies are developed to select among the degrees of freedom the controlled and the control variables so that an optimal operation is nearly obtained.

Given that thermal dynamics of VCR systems are typically slower than the mechanical dynamics, the bulk of the model complexity generally resides in the heat exchangers. Previous literature reviews [13][14] indicated that the bulk of the research efforts is focused on capturing two-phase flow dynamics in the heat exchangers while seeking a balance between simplicity and fidelity. For the purpose of this article, the four elements of the system will be classified into lumped parameters models. Lumped parameter models refer to models that apply lumped parameter assumptions to the entire heat exchanger or to particular fluid phases within the heat exchanger (i.e. individual lumped models for superheated vapor, two-phase fluid, and subcooled liquid), in this article, the term "lumped parameter model" includes approaches that model the heat exchanger as single-control volume or multiple (time-invariant) control volumes for each fluid phase. Most of the publications in the lumped parameter classification are early efforts, where computational simplicity is paramount to ensure feasible computation times, motivating modeling efforts with few dynamics equations and few (lumped) parameters [15].

Many analytical models are used to simulate steady-state performance of refrigeration systems, but do not predict performance during transient operation. This paper presents a method for predicting the cooling performance of VCR systems during transient and various ambient conditions based on established steady-state performance. In this work, we adopt a dynamic model of refrigeration system similar [16] but this is simplest with only four control volume.

This research is carried out in CIDESI Queretaro, for the National Laboratory for Cooling Technologies Research (LaNITeF).

The rest of the paper is structured as follow. In Section II, we review refrigeration cycle principles. Section III presents an explanation of model linearized on VCR systems. Section IV describes the balance of mass and energy of each element of the system, then the four ordinary differentials equations are modeling in Simulink of Matlab. Section V describes the validation of the modeling. Conclusions are found in Section VI.

II. REFRIGERATING SYSTEMS

Vapor-compressor refrigerating systems used with modern refrigerators vary considerably in capacity and complexity, depending on the refrigerating application. They are hermetically sealed and normally require no replenishment of refrigerant or oil during the appliance's useful life. Systems components must provide optimum overall performance and reliability at minimum cost. In addition, all safety requirements of the appropriate safety standard (e.g., IEC Standard 60335-2-24; UL Standard 250) must be met. The fully halogenated refrigerant R-12 was used in household refrigerators for many years. However, because of its strong ozone depletion property, appliance manufacturers have replaced R-12 with environmentally acceptable R134a or isobutene.

Design of refrigerating systems for refrigerators and freezers has improved because of new refrigerants and oils, wider use of aluminum, and smaller and more efficient motors, fans, and compressors. These refinements have kept the vapor-compression system in the best competitive position for household application.

A. Refrigerating circuit

Figure 1 shows the refrigeration cycle on p-h diagrams. The refrigerant evaporates entirely in the evaporator and produces the refrigerating effect. It is then extracted by the compressor at state point 1, compressor suction, and is compressed isentropically from state point 1 to 2. It is next condensed to liquid in the condenser, and the latent heat of condensation is rejected to the heat sink.

The liquid refrigerant, at state point 3, flows through and expansion valve, which reduces it to the evaporating pressure. In the ideal vapor compressor cycle, the throttling process at the expansion valve is the only irreversible process, usually indicated by a dotted line. Some of the liquid flashes into vapor and enters the evaporators at state point 4. The remaining liquid portion evaporates at the evaporating temperature, thus completing the cycle [17].

Note that energy enters the systems through the evaporator (heat load) and through the compressor (electrical input). Thermal energy is rejected to the ambient by the condenser and compressor shell. A portion of the capillarity tube is usually soldered to the suction line to form a heat exchanger. Cooling refrigerant in the capillarity tube with the suction gas increases capacity and efficiency.

A strainer-drier is usually placed ahead of the capillarity tube to remove foreign material and moisture. Refrigerant charges of 150 g or less are common.

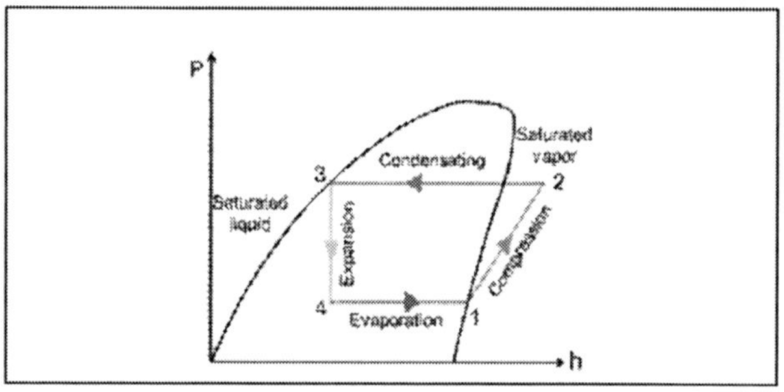

Figure 1. Diagram enthalpy vs Pressure.

A thermostat (or cold control) cycles the compressor to provide the desired temperatures in the refrigerator. During the off cycle, the capillarity tube allows pressure to equalize throughout the system [17][18].

III. LINEARIZED MODEL

Considering the dynamic response of commercial coolers based on vapor compression, various specialists have chosen to simplify the dynamic model on the basis of its ability to retain heat and the thermal resistance of its barriers [19][20]. These models consider the evaporator as a source of heat, which can inject or extract energy from the thermodynamic system to the inside of the cooler. Thus, C is considered as the thermal capacity of the volume inside the cooler and R heat resistance of its barriers, the linearized mathematical model is established as:

$$Q(t) = C\frac{dT_i}{dt} + [T_i - T_e]/R \tag{1}$$

Where $Q(t)$ is the heat injected or absorbed by the source in this case the evaporator, T_i and T_e are considered internal and external temperatures respectively. The model is easily recognizable as a first-order dynamic system and the internal temperature depends on the motor compressor angular speed, as shown in Figure 2.

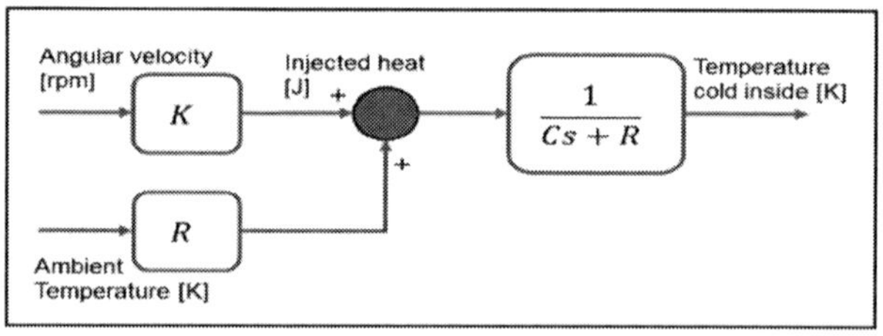

Figure 2. The Dynamic Model Analized Scheme.

In the same approach of the open-loop model, there are several control strategies implemented to regulate the internal temperature by applying a control law to manipulate the compressor speed.

As is the case with the thermodynamic model, there are several efforts where basic control strategies are implemented to regulate the internal temperature of the chiller based on the speed of the motor of the compressor control, such strategies are tuned considering the parameters of the linearized model [21][22]. A similar analysis is employed to define the conditions of the drivers hysteresis, [23][24]. A different approach found in literature, with respect to the modeling of the dynamics of the vapor compressor system implemented using heuristic algorithms, the most typical tool in Neural Networks [25], fuzzy logic, [26] and genetic algorithms [27]. The disadvantage of these heuristic models is that their internal variables do not have any physical interpretation, although very well solve the problem of the internal temperature regulation whereas the non-linearity which affects the performance of the model linearized described above.

IV. Dynamic Model of the VCR System

A. Energy Conservation Law

Because the refrigeration cycle of a reciprocating refrigerating system is a closed cycle, if the system is operated in continuous and steady state (i.e., in an equilibrium state), according to the principle of continuity of mass and energy balance, the mass flow rates of refrigerant flowing through the evaporator, compressor, condenser and expansion or float valve must all be equal. Also, the total amount of energy supplied to the refrigeration system must be approximately equal to the total energy rejected from the system.

A continuous and steady state means that the flow is continuous, and the properties of the refrigerant at any point in the refrigeration system do not vary over time. Therefore, during the design of a refrigeration system, the system components selected should have equal or approximately equal mass flow rates of refrigerant at stable conditions [17][28].

A balance of energy (first law of thermodynamics), combined with mass conservation in the control volume provides the following equation;

$$\dot{Q}+\dot{W}=\dot{m}\left[\left(h_o-h_i\right)+\frac{v_o^2-v_i^2}{2}+g\left(z_o-z_i\right)\right] \quad (2)$$

The equation (2) $\dot{Q}$ is transferred to the system by the surrounding heat flow, $\dot{W}$ is the work power performed by the electric motor of the compressor, h is enthalpy function that is associated with the sum of the internal energy and the work flow, $u + Pv$, the linear kinetic energy $v^2/2$ and potential energy gravity gz of the fluid stream. The subscripts i and o represent the conditions of entry and exit, respectively. In the absence of appreciable variations of kinetic and potential energy the equation above reduces to:

$$\dot{Q}+\dot{W}+\dot{Q}_{Pi}=\dot{m}_r c_p\left(T_o-T_i\right) \quad (3)$$

This relationship is grounded on the consideration that all variables distributions along in the finite volume (control volume) are homogeneous, and it is going to be applied for each one of the control volume from the four stage of the refrigeration cycle. In this equation, $\dot{m}_r$ is the mass of refrigerant in circulation, c_{pi} is the specific heat of the refrigerant at room temperature, which is considered constant, (Table 1). Q_{Pi} represents the heat loss or heat generated by the system and corresponds to the Newton's law of cooling, dT/dt is the speed with which the object cools for this analysis represents the change in temperature of the refrigerant, [29].

$$Q_{Pi}=C_{Ti}\frac{dT_i}{dt}+\frac{\left(T_i-T_a\right)}{R_{Ti}} \quad (4)$$

In the volume control 1, C_{Ti} is the thermal capacitance to the interior of the space confined to the evaporator element and for other elements is the capacitance of the material, which can be also expressed $C_{Ti}=mc_p$, thus, m is the mass of the elements and $c_{p,m}$ is considered the heat capacity of the material with which is manufactured elements, T_i is the temperature inside the system, and T_a is the ambient temperature. This model enthalpy is considered like ideal gas;

$$\Delta h=c_p\left(T_o-T_i\right) \quad (5)$$

Figure 3 shows the physical quantities involving to the system analyzed.

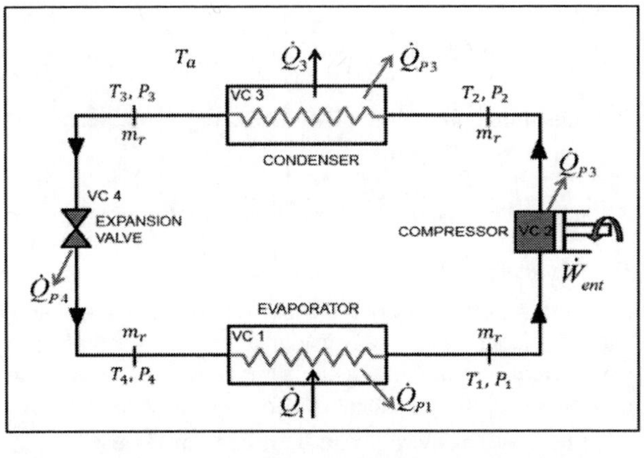

Figure 3. The Dynamic Model Analyzed Scheme.

The following simplifications are considered: (i) the physical properties related to the refrigerant is considered uniform in the heat exchanger transversal section, (ii) the refrigerant liquid and vapor phases are in thermodynamic equilibrium, (iii) the heat exchangers have a perfect thermal insulation, (iv) the axial heat conduction in the pipes is not taken into account.

B. Evaporator Mathematical Model

To obtain this model $\dot{Q}=0$ as the heat removed by the refrigerant from the confined space which is also known as thermal load, the work $\dot{W}=0$, equation 3 and 4, arises:

$$\dot{Q}_1 + \dot{Q}_{P1} = \dot{m}_r c_p (T_1 - T_4) \tag{6}$$

Substituting into (4), Newton's law of cooling and ordering terms is obtained;

$$\frac{dT_{R1}}{dt} = T_1\left(\frac{c_p \dot{m}_r}{C_{T1}} - \frac{1}{C_{T1}R_{T1}}\right) - T_4\frac{c_p \dot{m}_r}{C_{T1}} + \frac{T_a}{C_{T1}R_{T1}} - \frac{\dot{Q}_1}{C_{T1}} \tag{7}$$

C. Mathematical Model of Compressor

Motor shaft dynamics are modeled from an angular momentum balance between the driving and braking torques. The torque-speed characteristics of the motor itself are obtained from manufacturer´s data. From these, the driving torque and speed to the compressor are known.

For this model, the following hypothesis is established; there is no friction on the compressor, is an adiabatic process $\dot{Q}_1 = 0$. The other variables set for analysis.

$$\dot{W}_C = \frac{n}{(n-1)}\eta_p V_c \omega_c p_1\left[1-\left(\frac{p_2}{p_3}\right)^{\frac{n-1}{n}}\right] \tag{8}$$

The torque provided by the motor of the compressor $\dot{W} = \dot{T}_R$ and ω is the angular velocity of the shaft of the electric motor of the compressor. Equation (3) and (4), arises;

$$\dot{W}_R + \dot{Q}_{P2} = \dot{m}_r c_p (T_2 - T_1) \tag{9}$$

Substituting into (4) to (8) and ordering terms, gets;

$$\frac{dT_2}{dt} = -T_1\frac{c_p \dot{m}_r}{C_{T2}} + T_2\left(\frac{c_p \dot{m}_r}{C_{T2}} - \frac{1}{C_{T2}R_{T2}}\right) + \frac{T_a}{C_{T2}R_{T2}} - \frac{\dot{W}_1}{C_{T2}} \tag{10}$$

D. Mathematical Model of Condenser

In this element, only the superheat vapor is considered and the vapor phase is considered to be in the thermal equilibrium and moving at the same velocity. Work is not performed in this element $\dot{W}=0$, $\dot{Q}=0$ it is the heat released into the environment. It arises from (3) and (4);

$$\dot{Q}_3 + \dot{Q}_{P3} = \dot{m}_r c_p (T_3 - T_2) \tag{11}$$

Substituting (4) into (10) and ordering terms, gets;

$$\frac{dT_3}{dt} = -T_2\left(\frac{c_p \dot{m}_r}{C_{T3}}\right) + T_3\left(\frac{c_p \dot{m}_r}{C_{T3}} - \frac{1}{C_{T3}R_{T3}}\right) + \frac{T_a}{C_{T3}R_{T3}} - \frac{\dot{Q}_3}{C_{T3}} \tag{12}$$

E. Mathematical Model of the Expansion Valve

In this device there is no interaction of work and heat $\dot{W}=0$ and $\dot{Q}=0$, the expansion is isenthalpic. Then from (3) and (4), arises;

$$\dot{Q}_{P4} = \dot{m}_r c_p (T_3 - T_4) \tag{13}$$

Substituting (4) into (12) and ordering terms;

$$\frac{dT_4}{dt} = -T_3\left(\frac{c_p \dot{m}_r}{C_{T4}}\right) + T_4\left(\frac{c_p \dot{m}_r}{C_{T4}} - \frac{1}{C_{T4}R_{T4}}\right) + \frac{T_a}{C_{T4}R_{T4}} \tag{14}$$

F. State-space Representation of VCR System

In previous sections equations (7), (10), (12) and (14) has been presented as first-order linear ordinary differential equations, with the temperature of the refrigerant as the system output.

Whereas the following expressions in the matrix form, [30]:

$$\begin{aligned} \dot{T}(t) &= Ax(t) + Bu(t) \\ y(t) &= Cx(t) + Du(t) \end{aligned} \tag{15}$$

Equation (7), (10), (12) and (14) shall be replaced in (15):

$$\begin{bmatrix} \dot{T}_1 \\ \dot{T}_2 \\ \dot{T}_3 \\ \dot{T}_4 \end{bmatrix} = \begin{bmatrix} \left(\frac{c_p \dot{m}_r}{C_{T1}} - \frac{1}{C_{T1}R_{T1}}\right) & 0 & 0 & -\frac{c_p \dot{m}_r}{C_{T1}} \\ -\left(\frac{c_p \dot{m}_r}{C_{T2}}\right) & \left(\frac{c_p \dot{m}_r}{C_{T2}} - \frac{1}{C_{T2}R_{T2}}\right) & 0 & 0 \\ 0 & -\left(\frac{c_p \dot{m}_r}{C_{T3}}\right) & \left(\frac{c_p \dot{m}_r}{C_{T3}} - \frac{1}{C_{T3}R_{T3}}\right) & 0 \\ 0 & 0 & -\frac{c_p \dot{m}_r}{C_{T4}} & \left(\frac{c_p \dot{m}_r}{C_{T4}} - \frac{1}{C_{T4}R_{T4}}\right) \end{bmatrix} \begin{bmatrix} T_1 \\ T_2 \\ T_3 \\ T_4 \end{bmatrix}$$

$$+ \begin{bmatrix} \frac{1}{C_{T1}R_{T1}} & -\frac{1}{C_{T1}} & 0 & 0 \\ \frac{1}{C_{T2}R_{T2}} & 0 & -\frac{1}{C_{T2}} & 0 \\ \frac{1}{C_{T3}R_{T3}} & 0 & 0 & -\frac{1}{C_{T3}} \\ \frac{1}{C_{T4}R_{T4}} & 0 & 0 & 0 \end{bmatrix} \begin{bmatrix} T_a \\ \dot{Q}_1 \\ \dot{T}_R \\ \dot{Q}_3 \end{bmatrix}$$

$$y(t) = \begin{bmatrix} 1 & 0 & 0 & 0 \\ 0 & 1 & 0 & 0 \\ 0 & 0 & 1 & 0 \\ 0 & 0 & 0 & 1 \end{bmatrix} \begin{bmatrix} T_1 \\ T_2 \\ T_3 \\ T_4 \end{bmatrix} + 0$$

V. VALIDATION OF THE MODELING

The mathematical model obtained in the previous section for the prediction of dynamic behavior was coded in Matlab Simulink. The typical values of input parameters have been presented in Table 1 the input parameters include refrigerant type, ambient temperature and the initial temperature of the compartment, etc. The values of c_{pi} of the refrigerant were defined according the average of the phase in regard on p vs h diagram.

Considering the thermodynamic cycle starts-up when the system is powered by the angular speed of the electric motor of the compressor, the flow of the refrigerant quickly tends to a permanent state, it can be noted that the refrigerant tends to decrease its temperature at the evaporator element, trying to keep the relationship of equilibrium of Pressure and Temperature [31].

TABLE I. VALUES OF MATLAB ALGORITHM OF SIMULIK PROGRAM

C_{p1}=1330	J/kg-K	C_{T1}=4500	J/K	R_{T1}=0.090	K/W
C_{p2}=1400	J/kg-K	C_{T2}=2500	J/K	R_{T2}=0.025	K/W
C_{p3}=1138	J/kg-K	C_{T3}=1250	J/K	R_{T3}=0.048	K/W
C_{p4}=1318	J/kg-K	C_{T4}=500	J/K	R_{T4}=3.20	K/W
Q_1=195	W	T_a=298	K	m_r=0.000035	kg/s
Q_3=-200	W	T_R=5	W		

The following figures show the dynamic evolution of the refrigeration cycle of two important variables: temperature and pressure starting from ambient temperature; then, it approaches the steady state.

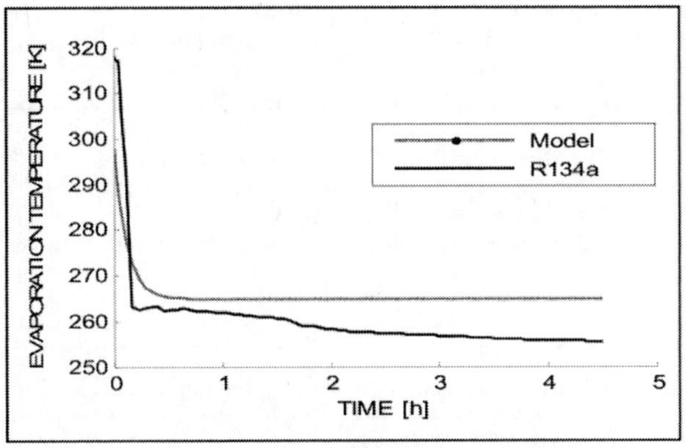

Figure 4. Behavor of the temperature of the evaporation system.

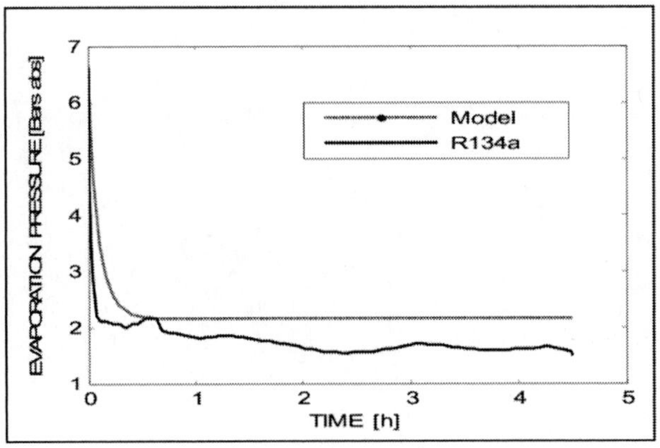

Figure 5. Transient temperature profile from development model.

Figure 4 shows the evolution of temperatures behaves in the compartment of the refrigerator, the model is compared with Embraco Data [31], using R-143a, it can be observed takes about 10 minutes in the transient state, then the room temperature reaches the steady state operation.

Figure 5 shows the evolution the behave pressure of the refrigerant in the evaporator when it flow thought the length tube, we can appreciates the same approach considering it begin from external temperature. Figure 5 shows the results when the thermodynamic cycle has been developed on the diagram pressure versus enthalpy, explained in section II.

A reasonable agreement between model and measure values from Embraco Data [31] was observed for the whole start-up period, during the first 5 minutes, the pressure below from 6.5 bars to 2.2 bars, and then it tends to decrease slowly until to reach steady state operation.

VI. CONCLUSION

In the present work, a methodology has been developed to model transient behavior of the refrigerator. This would act as foundation to transient model of domestic refrigerator, using lumped transient model. This methodology, based on lumped parameters model will reduce the overall cycle time in predicting the transient compartment temperature and will also decrease the experimental effort.

The results presented in this paper agree qualitatively with temperature time evolution shown other papers. Calculation for transient analysis of domestic refrigerators, obtained with the computer program here presented, will further validate with experimental data in near future.

Therefore, it is considered that it is a good starting point for the study of cooling systems applying state variables. The first strategy will be the vector by the feedback of states since becoming a linear approximation; however, you can see that there are nonlinearities, so it is contemplated in the near future to implement an algorithm control parameters identification and adaptive control, which will be validated with experimentation in the facilities of LaNITeF.

ACKNOWLEDGMENT

The authors thank the Mexican Council for Science and Technology (CONACYT) for its support of both students scholarships No. (599179, 492895), and the LaNITeF Consolidation Project as well.

Thanks also to the CIDESI campus Estado de Mexico for the technology availability and collaboration.

REFERENCES

[1] G. L. Wedekind, B. L. Bhatt, and B. T. Beck, "A system mean void fraction model for predicting various transient phenomena associated with two phase evaporating and condensing flows," International Journal of Multiphase Flow, vol. 4, pp. 97–114, 1978.

[2] M. Dhar and W. Soedel, "Transient analysis of a vapour-compression refrigeration system parts 1 and 2," In: 15th International Congress of Refrigeration, 1979.

[3] J. Chi and D. A. Didion, "Simulation model of the transient performance of a heat pump," Int J Refrigeration, vol. 5(3), pp. 176–84, 1982.

[4] J. W. MacArthur and E. W. Grald, "Prediction of cyclic heat pump performance with a fully distributed model and a comparison with experimental data," ASHRAE Transactions, pp. 1159-78, 1987.

[5] S. Bendapudi and J. E. Braun, "A Review of Literature on Dynamic Models of Vapour Compression Equipment," Technical Report HL2002-8. Ray W. Herrick Laboratories, Purdue University, 2002.

[6] B. P. Rasmussen and A. G. Alleyne, "Dynamic Modeling and Advanced Control of Air Conditioning and Refrigeration Systems," Dept. of Mechanical Engineering, University of Illinois, 2005.

[7] L. C. Schurt, Ch. J. L. Hermes, and A. T. Neto, "A model-driven multivariable controller for vapor compression refrigeration systems". IJR, vol. 32, pp. 1672-182, 2009.

[8] X. He, S. Liu, and H. H. Asada, "Modeling of vapor compression cycles for multivariable feedback control of HVAC systems," ASME Journal of Dynamic Systems, Measurement and Control, vol. 119 (2), pp. 183-191, 1997.

[9] L. C. Schurt, C. J. L. Hermes, and A. T. Neto, "A model driven multivariable controller for vapor compressor refrigeration system," International Journal of Refrigeration, vol. 23(7), pp. 588-595, 2009.

[10] B. P. Rasmussen, A. Alleyne, C. Bullard, P. Hrnjak, and N. Miller, "Control-Oriented Modeling and Analysis of Automotive Transcritical AC System Dynamics," Proc. American Control Conf., pp. 3111-3116, 2002.

[11] J. B. Jensen and S. Skogestad, "Optimal operation of simple refrigeration cycles". Computers and Chemical Engineering vol. 31, pp. 712–721, 2007a.

[12] J. B. Jensen and S. Skogestad, "Optimal operation of simple refrigeration cycles," Part II Seleccion of controlled variables.

[13] Computers and Chemical Engineering, vol. 31, pp. 1590–1601, 2007b.

[14] J. Lebrun and J. P. Bourdouxhe, "Reference guide for dynamic models of HVAC equipment," Project 738-TPR, 1998.

[15] S. Bendapudi and J. E. Braun, "Development and Validation of a mechanistic, dynamic model for a vapor compression centrifugal chiller," Report No. 4036-4 ASHRAE, Atlanta G.A. 2002b.

[16] B. P. Rasmussen, "Dynamic Modeling for Vapor Compression systems," Part I literature review. HVAC and Research, pp. 934-950, 2012.

[17] J. V. C. Vargas and J. A. R. Parise, "Simulation in transient regime of a heat pump with closed-loop and on-off control," IJR, vol. 18 (4), pp. 235-243, May 1995.

[18] Handbook-Refrigeration, ASHRAE, Chapter 9, pp. 424-430, 2000.

[19] Handbook-Refrigeration, ASHRAE Chapter 17, pp. 262-264, 2010.

[20] M. Stadler, W. Krause, and M. Sonnenschein, "Modelling and evaluation of control schemes for anhancing load shift of electricity demand for cooling devices," Enviromental Modelling and Software, vol. 24, Issue 2, pp. 285-295, 2009.

[21] M. Ouszzane and Z. Aidoun, "Model development and numerical procedure for detailed ejector analysis and design," Applied Thermal Eng., vol. 23(18), pp. 2337-51, 2003.

[22] J. Dieckmann, D. Westphalen, W. Murphy, P. Sikkirm, and C. Rieger, "Application of a variable speed compressor to a residential no-frost freezer," TIAX., Jan 27, 2004.

[23] Secop, 2011, SLV Compressors with 105N46XX series controller, [online]. Available from: https://www.secop.com/updates/news-secop-slv-compressors-with-105n46xx-series-controller/ 2017.07.25

[24] W. R. Chang, D. Liu, S. G. Chen, and Wu, "The components and control methods for implementation of inverter-controlled refrigerators / Freezer," Purdue University, N. Y., 2004.

[25] J. M. León, Design of automated reactor cooling system, University of Carabobo. Venezuela. 2003.

[26] M. Aydinalp, V. I. Ugursal, and A. S. Fung, "Modeling of the space and domestic hotwater heating energy consumption in the residential sector using neural networks," Applied Energy, Elsevier, vol. 71, pp. 87-110, 2002.

[27] M. Knezic, Fuzzy Logic Apparatus Control, United States Patern, Number 5,261,247, 1993.

[28] M. Mraz, "The Design of Intelligent Control of a Kitchen Refrigerator," Mathematic and Computing in Simulation, Elsevier, vol. 56, No. 3, pp. 259-267, 2001.

[29] W. Kenneth and E. R. Donald, Thermodynamics, 6th ed, Mc Graw Hill: Spain, pp. 190-192, 2001.

[30] W. Bolton, Mechatronics, electronic control in the mechanical and electrical engineering systems, 5th ed, Alfaomega: Mexico D. F., pp. 261-264, May 2013.

[31] K. Ogata, Modern control engineering, 5th ed. Pearson, pp. 136-139, 2010.

[32] Embraco, technical information. [Online]. Available from: http://www.embraco.com/DesktopModules/DownloadsAdmin/Arquivos/xd0vsAjtYw.pdf 2017.09.05

Analysis of the Dynamic Behavior of the Temperature Distribution Inside a Domestic Refrigerator

Jesús Hernán Pérez Vázquez, Carlos Alexander Nuñez Martín, Helen Janeth Zuniga Osorio
Engineering Center for Industrial Development (CIDESI)
National Research Laboratory on Cooling Technology (LaNITeF)
Santiago de Querétaro, Querétaro, México
e-mail: jperez@posgrado.cidesi.edu.mx,
e-mail: cnunez@posgrado.cidesi.edu.mx,
e-mail: hzuniga@posgrado.cidesi.edu.mx

Ottmar Rafael Uriza Gosebruch
Engineering Center for Industrial Development (CIDESI)
P02 Eolic Energy Project
Cd. de México, México
e-mail: ottmar.uriza@cidesi.edu.mx

Celso Eduardo Cruz González
Engineering Center for Industrial Development (CIDESI)
Advanced Manufacturing Department
Cd. de México, México
e-mail: ecruz@cidesi.edu.mx

***Abstract*— A mathematical model to describe the dynamics of heat extraction in a domestic refrigerator is exposed in this document. The concerned model is based on the Newton's Law for Cooling as a boundary condition (walls that isolate the volume of the box and keep the low energy level) for the Fourier Heat Equation, which is used to describe the energetic exchange among the mass nodes considered from the finite volumes concept. The model was codified through Matlab and used for simulation and validation with experimental results. The simulation results add information to validate that the temperature is not homogenous inside the appliance. The information provided helps to understand the evolution of temperature changes, assuming a homogeneous environment and different ratios of thermal capacity.**

Keywords- heat exchange; thermal diffusivity; finite volume.

I. Introduction

The implementation of new technologies for the refrigeration industry has increased significantly in recent years. The purpose of these new implementations was to address different issues, such as energy expenditure and the impact on the environment [1]. Cooling devices are mainly used for conservation of perishable foods, making them indispensable for the conservation of large volumes of food, for a commercial level, and in small quantities, for domestic consumption [2]. This article focuses on the exchange of energy inside a domestic refrigerator and the relation between energy consumption and thermal load contained in the refrigerator chamber [3], leading to better food conservation and reducing the negative environmental impact. The relevant understanding of the dynamics of energy can be achieved by formulating a mathematical model, using the law of cooling of Newton and the equation of heat of Fourier, and by solving both using the method of finite volumes.

The present work is structured as follows: Section II mentions the basic concepts to detail the proposed theories and the expected effects. Section III presents the mathematical model developed and the results obtained from the simulation. In addition, it provides an early interpretation of the process of energy exchange between mass along the internal volumes. Section IV explains the results generated by the simulations and their possible effect in the refrigeration cycle. Finally, Section V discusses the final conclusions of this first stage of the research developed.

II. Basic Concepts

To determine the mathematical model, certain conditions are assumed for the rest of this text, namely that the environment temperature is homogeneous, and the thermodynamic parameters of materials are constant. Previous considerations are proposed to generate a linear model. Newton's Law of Cooling models the transfer of heat between the environment and the internal volume, considering a thin layer of insulation [7]. Fourier's heat equation was used for the transfer of energy in the internal volume, ignoring the gas flow inside the cold chamber. The elements used as thermal loads were air and water. The Fourier heat equation, mainly used for conduction of heat energy between solid materials, can also be solved for gases, considering that the fluid will not have any movement, and only focusing our interest on the mass confined the volume protected by the insulator [10]. Newton's cooling law is used as the boundary condition that simulates the insulation from the environment, adding perturbation to the refrigeration cycle [8]. The outside temperature is considered uniform at the surface of each wall.

Two states of thermal load, empty and full, are considered: 0% of thermal energy stored (empty), to determinate the temperature evolution and the energy decrease along time [9]. 100% of accumulated thermal energy (full), to show the difference between the absence of load in the refrigeration cycle [11].

A. Characteristics of the model

The transfer medium in the inside of the chamber, in 0% of thermal load and a time of 0 sec, is considered a homogeneous mixture (air), with a thermal conductivity of 0.024 w / m °K. The movement of air is not considered. The internal energy is extracted, and it is expelled to the outside. The evaporator is maintained on to reduce the energy of the air in a first empty state.

The system dynamic is altered when the thermal load changes its state from empty to full. By modifying the thermodynamic properties, the extraction of heat of the thermal equilibria changes. It is considered that the properties of water in its liquid state can provide an approximation of the behavior of food in refrigeration.

For purposes of a first approximation, only two possible states of the thermal load are considered, considering that the space to extract the energy could be empty or totally full. As a future work, an adjustment may be made to consider different middle operation points.

The different material characteristics used in the model are presented in TABLE I:

TABLE I. VALUES USED IN THE MATHEMATICAL MODEL

Symbol	Characteristics	
	Name	***Unity***
α	Thermal diffusivity	K/ρC
K	Thermal conductivity	W/m °C
ρ	Density	Kg/m^3
C	Specific Heat	J/Kg °C
$\Delta_{x,y,z}$	Delta	m
Δ_t	Time Differential	s
V_{nodo}	Node volume	m^3
$\dot{Q}$	Generated Heat	W

B. Theoretical Proposal

For this investigation, the model was focused on the internal volume of refrigeration (evaporator output), considering that its motion has a static behavior and is described by the following dynamics, as observed in equation (1).

$$\dot{Q}_{conducción} = -kA\frac{dT}{dx} \quad (1)$$

According to the elapsed time, and the amount of energy that the heat source can emit, the characteristics vary, which are the thermal conductivity, the temperature gradient and the volume. In order to obtain a linear approximation, constant properties are considered throughout the duration of the simulation.

C. Volume Analysis

Considering that the objective is to describe the thermal distribution in space of the chamber, three space dimensions are considered, obtaining the mathematical model indicated in equation (2).

The volume of each material is considered. The assumption that there are no spaces of different materials is applied. All possible volumes in the total space are in prismatic form, causing the transfer of heat between the formed nodes similar to a solid. The only path of heat transference is in the direction of the three space dimension.

$$T_{i,j,k}^{n+1} = \alpha \cdot \Delta t \left(\frac{\partial^2 T}{\partial x^2} + \frac{\partial^2 T}{\partial y^2} + \frac{\partial^2 T}{\partial z^2} + \frac{1}{k}\dot{Q}''_{i,j,k} \right) + T_{i,j,k}^{n-1} \quad (2)$$

Solving the dynamic model helped to generate the distribution of temperature as a function of time and space.

The heat source is the evaporator, but the sign of its effect in the system is negative, because of the idea of extracting energy from the interior, instead of inserting energy from the exterior. The interaction of energy between the evaporator and the outside is not explained in this document.

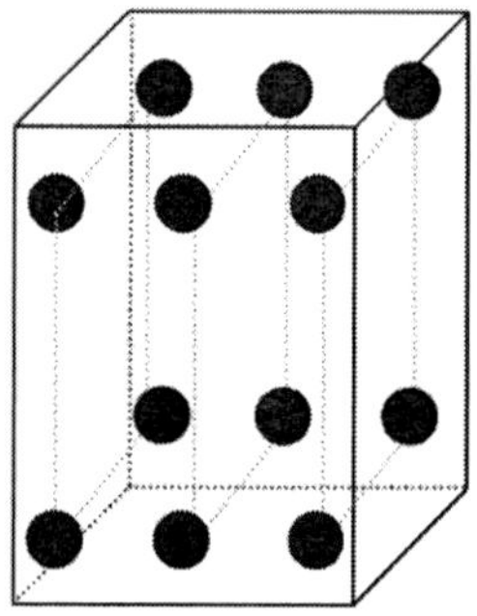

Figure 1. Distribution of nodes in the space of the cold chamber.

In Figure 1, the temperature nodes inside the chamber are shown.

III. MATHEMATICAL MODEL AND SIMULATION RESULTS

The process of data acquisition requires a commercial refrigerator with linear compressor, with the following characteristics: 132 watts 60 Hz and 313 watts 150 Hz, representing 0% and 100% thermal load, respectively.

In addition, the width of the insulating wall (polyurethane) has a value of 0.05 m. The energy entering the cold chamber was 1.64 W, this energy being added to the heat generated (extraction of energy from the evaporator). The minimum value of the evaporator in an empty state, and it is selected assuming that no thermal load with greater conductivity than water leads to minimum work from the evaporator. The interaction of energy between temperature nodes causes an increase or decrease in energy of every surrounding node.

A. Operation of the model

The temperature behavior should be radial with the center in the evaporator output. Every node will have a limit of energy extraction coinciding with the phase change energy of every material.

The simulation was generated proposing the space of the refrigerator as empty, without shelves any object or product inside.

As explained in Section II, only rectangular heat fluctuation is considered. It is for this reason that no other geometric flow is considered.

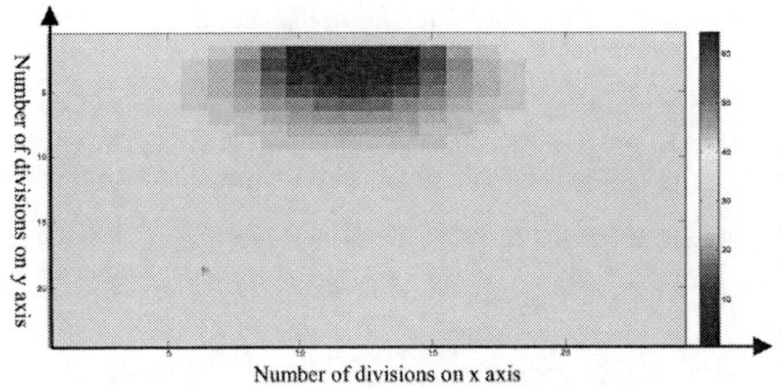

Figure 2. Behavior of the temperature distribution in the domestic refrigerator vacuum

The empiricial behavior is coherent with the theoretical radial propagation, hence, the evaporator location to show the lowest values in temperature as seen in Figure 2. Figure 3 shows the same behavior as Figure 2, but with a transversal view on the z axis, divided into 9 different instants. The subfigures 1, 2 3 are the first layers and show a considerable decrease in the internal energy, in layers 4, 5, 6 they show a higher energy, but a decrease in the lower part of the chamber, because the density of the air increases when temperature decreases.

The solution of finite volumes determines the zones of the refrigeration cycle depending on the thermal load and the percentage of use of the compressor, empty or full as mentioned previously, generating two zones. In Figure 4, the red zone indicates that after working at 100 percent and with a total time of 12 hours (simulated), the system does not reach steady state. However, with thermal load in 0%, the system stabilizises.

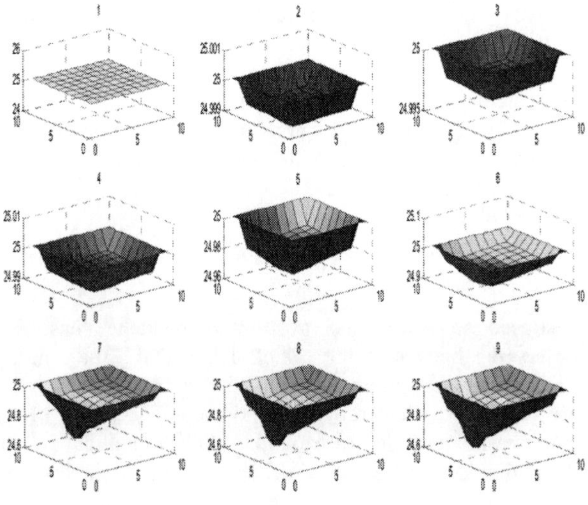

Figure 3. Behavior of the temperatures according to the height of the refrigerator.

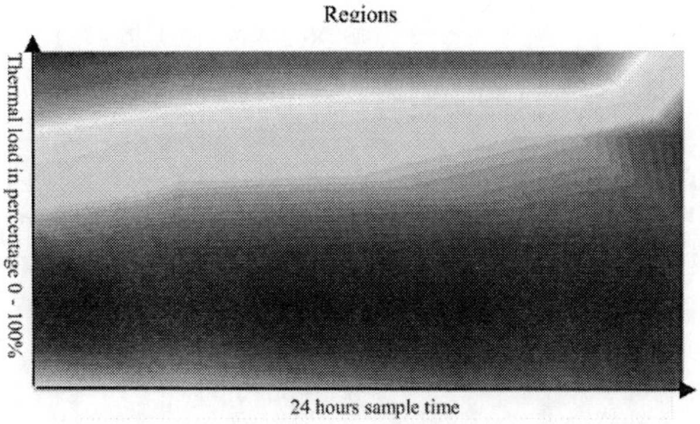

Figure 4. Distribution of the energy inside the cold chamber with different thermal loads.

The results will be further analized in Section IV.

IV. ANALYSIS OF RESULTS

Based on the concept of finite volume, the Fourier's equation (proposed model) solved in finite differences considering the sub-node strategy, maintains a dynamic behavior similar to a first order system for all its nodes. The dynamic obtained with the experimental characterization represents a behavior consistent with the empirical results. Since the model proposed in finite differences, in each iteration, is fed by temperature data at the output of the evaporator inside the cold chamber (sensor available in the refrigerator), the stabilization time of the model is consistent with the experimental results. However, the theoretical values of the constants require adjustments; to reduce the deviations in a permanent regime. Based on the results obtained from the tests, 4 critical zones were chosen to analyze the dynamic response due to the thermal load, as well as the dynamic response due to the speed of the compressor. In each zone, the corresponding dynamic poles are calculated from each time constant. Considering the poles obtained for the 4 regions of the load-velocity space, the errors with respect to the theoretical values must be considerably reduced.

V. CONCLUSIONS

Based on the results, a strong dependence has been observed between the coefficients of the model (thermodynamic properties) and the control variables that are regulated in the refrigerator device. The speed of the compressor and the distribution and magnitude of the thermal load inside the refrigerator are variables that contribute to modify the temperature evolution of the system. The non-linearity of the phenomenon must be considered when modifying the value of the poles in the model and is supported by the improvement of the results.

ACKNOWLEDGMENT

The authors thank the Mexican Council for Science and Technology (CONACYT) for its support for both students scholarships (437556, 555423), and the LaNITeF Consolidation Project as well. Thanks also to the Mexican Innovation Centers for Energy Technology (CEMIE) for the support and equipment access through the P02 Eolic Energy Project and the LICORE company for the technology availability and collaboration.

REFERENCES

[1] P. V. Hernán et al., "Structural model of a domestic refrigeration appliance" AMCA 2016.

[2] P. V. Hernán and R. Eloy, "Structural model of the internal temperature distribution in a cold chamber". *Congreso Nacional 2016 PICYT, Leon Guanajuato.*

[3] P. Hernán, R. Eloy and N. Alexander, "Mathematical simplification of the heat extraction of a domestic refrigerator". Congress of Young Researchers, Queretaro 2016.

[4] F. Belmant et al., "Analysis of the temperature stratification of a no-frost domestic refrigerator whit bottom mount configuration" Applied Thermal Engineering 65 (2014) Peg. 299-307.

[5] Jara Nelson et al., "Dynamic model for the study of the application of the refrigeration renewal plan in Colombia" Universidad Salesiana Ecuador, 2016.

[6] J. Nelson and I. Cesar, "Sistemas de refrigeración doméstica – Estado del arte de las mejoras en la eficiencia energética" Universidad Salesiana Ecuador , 2016.

[7] S. A. Tassou et al., "A review of emerging technologies for food refrigeration applications" Applied Thermal Engineering 30, 2010,pag. 263,276.

[8] C. E Vincet and M. K. Heun, "Thermoeconomic analisys & design of domestic refrigeration systems" domestic use energy Conference 2006.

[9] A. Bromberg et al., "Tips and techniques that do not harm the environment for the technical service of equipment with refrigerators" Mainstream Engineering Corporation, Rockledge, Florida. https://www.epatest.com/608/manual/Manual_SP.htm.

[10] J. M. Belman, Analysis of the flow and temperature distribution inside the comportment of a small refrigerator, 2016.

[11] E. Björk and B. Palm, Refrigerant mass charge distribution in a domestic refrigerator. Part II: Steady state conditions, 2008